Spanish

PHRASE FINDER

HarperCollins*Publishers*

CONSULTANT
Isabel Rugama

First published 1993
Copyright © HarperCollins Publishers
Reprint 10 9 8 7 6 5 4
Printed in Great Britain

ISBN 0 00-470283-2

Your *Collins Gem Phrase Finder* is designed to help you locate the exact phrase you need in any situation, whether for holiday or business. If you want to adapt the phrases, we have made sure that you can easily see where to substitute your own words (you can find them in the dictionary section), and the clear, alphabetical, two-colour layout gives you direct access to the different topics.

The *Phrase Finder* includes:

- Over 70 topics arranged alphabetically from **ACCOMMODATION** to **WORK**. Each phrase is accompanied by a simple pronunciation guide which ensures that there's no problem over pronouncing the foreign words.

- Practical hints and useful vocabulary highlighted in boxes. Where the English words appear first in the box, this indicates vocabulary you may need. Where the red Spanish words appear first, these are words you are more likely to see written on signs and notices.

WORDS APPEARING IN BLACK ARE ENGLISH WORDS	WORDS APPEARING IN RED ARE SPANISH WORDS

- Possible phrases you may hear in reply to your questions. The foreign phrases appear in red.

- A clearly laid-out 5000-word dictionary: English words appear in black and Spanish words appear in red.

- A basic grammar section which will enable you to build on your phrases.

It's worth spending time before you embark on your travels just looking through the topics to see what is covered and becoming familiar with what might be said to you.

Whatever the situation, your *Phrase Finder* is sure to help!

*Spelling and pronouncing Spanish are easy once you know the few basic rules. This book has been designed so that as you read the pronunciation of the phrases you can follow the Spanish. This will help you to recognize the different sounds and give you a feeling for the rhythm of the language. The syllable to be stressed is marked in **heavy italics** in the pronunciation. Here are a few rules you should know:*

SPANISH	SOUNDS LIKE	EXAMPLE	PRONUNCIATION
■ CA	*ka*	cama	***ka****ma*
CO	*ko*	con	*kon*
CU	*ku*	cubo	***koo****bo*
■ CE	*the*	cena	***the****na*
CI	*thee*	cine	***thee****-ne*
■ GA	*ga*	gato	***ga****to*
GO	*go*	algo	***al****go*
GU	*goo*	algún	*al-****goon***
■ GE	*khe*	gente	***khen****te*
GI	*khee*	giro	***khee****ro*
■ J	*kh*	jueves	***khwe****-bes*
■ LL	*ly*	llamo	***lya****mo*
■ Ñ	*ny*	señor	*se****nyor***
■ UA	*w*	cual	*kwal*
UE	*w*	vuelva	***bwel****ba*
■ V	*b*	vuelva	***bwel****ba*
■ Z	*th*	zaragosa	*thara-****go****tha*

H is silent: **hora** **o**-ra, **hola** **o**-la.

R is rolled and **RR** even more so.

*In Spanish, vowels (**a**, **e**, **i**, **o**, **u**) have only one sound. When you find two together, pronounce both of them in quick succession as in* **aceite** *a-****the****-ee-te.*

■ **ALPHABET**

6

If you haven't booked your accommodation, check with the local tourist office to see if they have a list of hotels and guesthouses.

HOTEL	HOTEL	COMPLETO	FULL UP
HABITACIONES	ROOMS AVAILABLE	PENSIÓN	GUESTHOUSE

Do you have a list of accommodation with prices?
¿Tiene alguna guía de hoteles y apartamentos con precios?
tye-ne al-goona gee-a de o-teles ee a-parta-mentos kon prethyos

Is there a hotel here?
¿Hay algún hotel por aquí?
a-ee al goon o-tel por a-kee

Do you have any vacancies?
¿Tiene alguna habitación libre?
tye-ne al-goona abee-tathyon lee-bre

I'd like (to book) a room...   double
Quería (reservar) una habitación...   doble
ke-ree-a (re-serbar) oona abee-tathyon...   *do-ble*

single	with bath	with shower
individual	con baño	con ducha
eendee-beedwal	*kon banyo*	*kon doocha*

with a double bed   twin-bedded
con cama de matrimonio   con dos camas
kon kama de matree-monyo   *kon dos kamas*

with an extra bed for a child
con una cama supletoria para un niño
kon oona kama soo-pleto-rya para oon neenyo

A room that looks...   onto the garden   onto the sea
Una habitación que dé...   al jardín   al mar
oona abee-tathyon ke de...   *al khardeen*   *al mar*

We'd like two rooms next to each other
Quisiéramos dos habitaciones contiguas
kee-sye-ramos dos abee-tathyo-nes kontee-gwas

CONT...

We'd like to stay ... nights

Quisiéramos quedarnos ... noches
kee-sye-ramos kedar-nos ... no-ches

from ... till...

del ... al...
del ... al...

I will confirm...

Se lo confirmaré...
se lo konfeer-ma-re...

by letter

por escrito
por eskree-to

by fax

por fax
por faks

How much is it...?

¿Qué precio tiene...?
ke prethyo tye-ne...

per night

por noche
por no-che

per week

por semana
por se-ma-na

for half board

con media pensión
kon medya pensyon

full board

con pensión completa
kon pensyon kom-ple-ta

Is breakfast included

¿Es con desayuno?
es kon desa-yoo-no

Have you anything cheaper?

¿Tiene algo más barato?
tye-ne algo mas ba-ra-to

Can you suggest somewhere else?

¿Sabe usted de algún otro sitio?
sabe oosted de al-goon o-tro see-tyo

■ **YOU MAY HEAR**

Está todo ocupado

esta to-do okoo-pa-do
We're full up

¿Para cuántas noches?

para kwantas no-ches
For how many nights?

¿Su nombre, por favor?

soo nom-bre por fabor
Your name, please?

Por favor confírmelo...

por fabor konfeer-melo...
Please confirm...

por escrito
por eskree-to
by letter

por fax
por faks
by fax

■ **CAMPING** ■ **HOTEL** ■ **SIGHTSEEING & TOURIST OFFICE**

AMOUNT (of money)	EL IMPORTE
DELIVERY NOTE	EL ALBARÁN
ORDER	EL PEDIDO

I'd like to speak to someone in your accounts department

Quisiera hablar con alguien del departamento de contabilidad
kee-sye-ra a-blar kon al-gyen del depar-tamen-to de konta-bee-leedad

It's regarding invoice number...

Es con respecto a la factura número...
es kon res-pekto a la fak-toora noo-mero...

I think there is an error

Me parece que hay un error
me pa-rethe ke a-ee oon e-rror

We are still waiting for the invoice to be settled

Todavía estamos esperando a que se liquide la cuenta
toda-bee-a esta-mos espe-rando a ke se lee-keede la kwenta

Please supply a credit note and new invoice

Por favor, mande una nota de crédito y factura nueva
por fabor mande oona nota de kre-deeto ee fak-toora nweba

Please address the invoice to...

Por favor, emita la factura a nombre de...
por fabor e-meeta la fak-toora a nom-bre de...

The goods should be accompanied by a pro forma invoice

La mercancía debe ir acompañada de una factura pro forma
la merkan-thee-a debe eer a-kompa-nyada de oona fak-toora pro forma

Please state content and value of the consignment

Por favor, especifique el contenido y valor del envío
por fabor espe-theefee-ke el konte-needo ee balor del en-bee-o

■ **NUMBERS** ■ **TELEPHONE**

Most signs are in Spanish and English and you may go through the airport without having to speak any Spanish. Here are a few signs you will find useful to know. The blue customs channel is for EC citizens travelling within Europe who have no goods to declare.

LLEGADAS	ARRIVALS
CONTROL DE PASAPORTES	PASSPORT CONTROL
SOLO CUIDADANOS CEE	EEC PASSPORT HOLDERS
RECOGIDA DE EQUIPAJE	BAGGAGE RECLAIM
CONTROL DE ADUANAS	CUSTOMS CONTROL
NADA QUE DECLARAR	NOTHING TO DECLARE
OBJETOS PARA DECLARAR	ARTICLES TO DECLARE
GUARDERÍA	BABY ROOM
SALIDA	EXIT
ASEOS	TOILETS
PUNTO DE ENCUENTRO	MEETING POINT

Where is the luggage for the flight from...?
¿Dónde está el equipaje del vuelo de...?
don-de esta el ekee-pa-khe del bwelo de...

Where can I change some money?
¿Dónde se puede cambiar dinero?
don-de se pwe-de kambyar dee-nero

How do I/we get to the centre of *(name town)***...?**
¿Cómo se va al centro de...?
komo se ba al thentro de...

How much is the taxi fare...?   **into town**   **to the hotel**
¿Cuánto cuesta ir en taxi...?   al centro   al hotel
kwanto kwesta eer en taksee...   *al thentro*   *al o-tel*

Is there a bus to the city centre?
¿Hay algún autobús que vaya al centro?
a-ee al-goon owto-boos ke baya al thentro

■ BUS ■ LUGGAGE ■ METRO ■ TAXI

SALIDAS	DEPARTURES	FACTURACIÓN	CHECK-IN
TARJETA DE EMBARQUE	BOARDING CARD	VUELO	FLIGHT
PUERTA DE EMBARQUE	BOARDING GATE	RETRASO	DELAY

Where do I check in for the flight to...?
¿Dónde se factura para el vuelo de...?
don-de se fak-too-ra para el bwe-lo de...

Which is the departure gate for the flight to...?
¿Cuál es la puerta de embarque del vuelo para...?
kwal es la pwer-ta de em-bar-ke del bwe-lo para...

■ YOU MAY HEAR

El embarque se efectuará en la puerta número...
el em-bar-ke se efek-twa-ra en la pwer-ta noo-mero...
Boarding will take place at gate number...

Última llamada para los pasajeros del vuelo...
ool-teema lya-ma-da para los pasa-khe-ros del bwe-lo...
Last call for passengers on flight...

Su vuelo sale con retraso
soo bwe-lo sa-le kon re-tra-so
Your flight is delayed

■ IF YOU NEED TO CHANGE OR CHECK ON YOUR FLIGHT

I want to change / cancel my reservation
Quería cambiar / anular mi reserva
ke-ree-a kam-byar / anoo-lar mee re-ser-ba

I'd like to reconfirm my flight to...
Quisiera reconfirmar el vuelo a...
kee-sye-ra re-konfeer-mar el bwe-lo a...

Is the flight to ... delayed?
¿El vuelo para ..., sale con retraso?
el bwe-lo para ... sa-le kon re-tra-so

The Spanish alphabet treats ch, ll and ñ as separate letters. Below are the words used for clarification when spelling something out.

How do you spell it?
¿Cómo se escribe?
komo se es-kreebe

A as in Antonio, b as in Barcelona
A de Antonio, b de Barcelona
a de an-tonyo be de bar-the-lona

A	*a*	Antonio	*an-tonyo*
B	*be*	Barcelona	*bar-the-lona*
C	*the*	Carmen	*karmen*
CH	*che*	Chocolate	*choko-la-te*
D	*de*	Dolores	*dolo-res*
E	*e*	Enrique	*enree-ke*
F	*e-fe*	Francia	*franthya*
G	*khe*	Gerona	*khero-na*
H	*a-che*	Historia	*eesto-rya*
I	*ee*	Inés	*ee-nes*
J	*khota*	José	*koh-se*
K	*ka*	Kilo	*keelo*
L	*e-le*	Lorenzo	*lo-rentho*
LL	*e-lye*	Llobregat	*lyo-bregat*
M	*e-me*	Madrid	*madreed*
N	*e-ne*	Navarra	*na-barra*
Ñ	*e-nye*	Ñoño	*nyonyo*
O	*o*	Oviedo	*o-byedo*
P	*pe*	Paris	*parees*
Q	*koo*	Querido	*ke-reedo*
R	*e-re*	Ramón	*ramon*
S	*e-se*	Sábado	*sa-bado*
T	*te*	Tarragona	*tarra-gona*
U	*oo*	Ulises	*oo-lee-ses*
V	*oo-be*	Valencia	*ba-lenthya*
W	*oo-be do-ble*	Washington	*wo-sheengton*
X	*e-kees*	Xiquena	*ksee-kena*
Y	*ee gree-e-ga*	Yegua	*ye-gwa*
Z	*theta*	Zaragoza	*thara-gotha*

Yes	**No**	**OK!**
Sí	No	¡Vale!
see	*no*	*ba-le*

Please
Por favor
por fabor

Don't mention it
De nada
de nada

With pleasure!
Con mucho gusto!
kon moocho goosto

Thank you
Gracias
gra-thyas

Thanks very much
Muchas gracias
moochas gra-thyas

That's very kind
Muy amable
mwee a-ma-ble

Sir / Mr
Señor / Sr.
se-nyor

Madam / Mrs / Ms
Señora / Sra.
se-nyora

Miss
Señorita / Srta.
senyo-reeta

Excuse me! *(to catch attention)*
¡Oiga, por favor!
o-eega por fabor

Excuse me *(sorry)*
Perdone
perdo-ne

Pardon?
¿Cómo dice?
komo dee-the

I don't know
No sé
no se

I don't understand
No entiendo
no en-tyendo

Do you understand?
¿Entiende?
en-tyende

Do you speak English?
¿Habla usted inglés?
a-bla oosted een-gles

I speak very little Spanish
Hablo muy poco español
a-blo mwee poko espa-nyol

Could you repeat that, please?
¿Podría repetirlo, por favor?
podree-a re-peteer-lo por fabor

Do you mind if...?
¿Le importa si...?
le eem-porta see...

It doesn't matter
No importa
no eem-porta

CROSSING	LA TRAVESÍA
CRUISE	EL CRUCERO
CABIN	EL CAMAROTE

When is the next boat / ferry to...?
¿Cuándo sale el próximo barco / ferry para...?
*kwan*do *sa*-le el *prok*-seemo *bar*ko / ferry para...

Have you a timetable?
¿Tienen un horario?
tye-nen oon o-*ra*ryo

Is there a car ferry to...?
¿Hay transbordador de coches a...?
a-ee trans-bor-da*dor* de *ko*-ches a...

How much is a ticket...?
¿Cuánto cuesta el billete...?
*kwan*to *kwes*ta el bee-*lye*-te...

single
de ida
de *ee*da

return
de ida y vuelta
de *ee*da ee *bwel*ta

A tourist ticket
Un billete de clase turista
oon bee-*lye*-te de *kla*-se too-*rees*ta

How much is the crossing for a car and ... people?
¿Cuánto cuesta un pasaje para ... personas con coche?
*kwan*to *kwes*ta oon pa-*sa*khe para ... per-*so*nas kon *ko*-che

How long is the journey?
¿Cuánto dura el viaje?
*kwan*to *doo*ra el *bya*-khe

What time do we get to...?
¿A qué hora llegamos a...?
a ke *o*-ra lye-*ga*mos a...

Where does the boat leave from?
¿De dónde sale el barco?
de *don*-de *sa*-le el *bar*ko

When is the first / the last boat?
¿Cuándo sale el primer / el último barco?
*kwan*do *sa*-le el pree-*mer* / el *ool*-teemo *bar*ko

Is there somewhere to eat on the boat?
¿Hay cafetería / restaurante en el barco?
a-ee ka-fete-*ree*-a / restow-*ran*-te en el *bar*ko

> In Spanish the possessive (my, his, her, etc.) is generally not used
> with parts of the body, e.g.

My head hurts	*Me duele* la cabeza
My hands are dirty	*Tengo* las manos sucias

ankle	el tobillo	to-**bee**-lyo
arm	el brazo	**bra**-tho
back	la espalda	es-**pal**da
bone	el hueso	**we**so
chin	la barbilla	bar-**bee**-lya
ear	la oreja / el oído	o-**re**kha / o-**ee**do
elbow	el codo	**ko**do
eye	el ojo	**o**-kho
finger	el dedo	**de**do
foot	el pie	pye
hair	el pelo	**pe**lo
hand	la mano	**ma**no
head	la cabeza	ka-**be**tha
heart	el corazón	kora-**thon**
hip	la cadera	ka-**de**ra
joint	la articulación	artee-koola-**thyon**
kidney	el riñón	ree-**nyon**
knee	la rodilla	ro-**dee**lya
leg	la pierna	**pyer**-na
liver	el hígado	**ee**-gado
mouth	la boca	**bo**ka
nail	la uña	**oo**nya
neck	el cuello	**kwel**yo
nose	la nariz	na-**reez**
stomach	el estómago	es**to**-mago
throat	la garganta	gar-**gan**ta
thumb	el pulgar	pool-**gar**
toe	el dedo del pie	**de**do del pye
wrist	la muñeca	moo-**nye**ka

■ DOCTOR ■ PHARMACY

Can you help me?
¿Puede ayudarme?
pwe-de ayoo-darme

My car has broken down
Se me ha averiado el coche
se me a abe-ryado el ko-che

The car won't start
El coche no arranca
el ko-che no arran-ka

Can you give me a push?
¿Puede empujarme?
pwe-de em-pookharme

I've run out of petrol
Me he quedado sin gasolina
me e ke-dado seen gaso-leena

Is there a garage near here?
¿Hay un garage por aquí?
a-ee oon gara-khe por a-kee

The engine is overheating
El motor se calienta
el motor se ka-lyenta

The battery is flat
Se ha descargado la batería
se a deskar-gado la ba-teree-a

I need water
Necesito agua
ne-the-seeto agwa

It's leaking...
Pierde...
pyer-de...

petrol / oil / water
gasolina / aceite / agua
gaso-leena / athe-ee-te / agwa

I've a flat tyre
Tengo una rueda pinchada
tengo oona rweda peen-chada

I can't get the wheel off
No puedo quitar la rueda
no pwedo keetar la rweda

Can you tow me to the nearest garage?
¿Puede remolcarme hasta el garaje más próximo?
pwe-de remol-karme asta el gara-khe mas prok-seemo

Do you have parts for a (make of car)**...?**
¿Tiene repuestos para el...?
tye-ne re-pwestos para el...

The ... doesn't work properly (see CAR–PARTS)
El/La ... no funciona bien
el/la ... no foon-thyona byen

Can you replace the windscreen?
¿Me puede cambiar el parabrisas?
me pwe-de kambyar el para-breesas

■ **CAR–PARTS**

*A **bono-bus** card is usually valid for 10 journeys and must be stamped on board the bus. The word for coach is **el autocar**.*

Is there a bus to...?
¿Hay algún autobús que vaya a...?
*a-ee al-**goon** owto-**boos** ke ba*ya a...

Which bus goes to...?
¿Qué autobús va a...?
*ke owto-**boos** ba a...*

Where do I catch the bus to...?
¿Dónde se coge el autobús para...?
***don**-de se ko-khe el owto-**boos** para...*

We're going to...
Vamos a...
*ba*mos a...

Where do they sell bono-bus cards?
¿Dónde venden bono-buses?
***don**-de **ben**-den bono-**boos**es*

How much is it...?
¿Cuánto es...?
***kwan**to es...*

to the centre	to the beach	to the airport	to Toledo
al centro	a la playa	al aeropuerto	a Toledo
al **then**tro	a la **pla**ya	al a-ero-**pwer**to	a to-**le**do

How often are the buses to...?
¿Cada cuánto hay autobuses a...?
***ka**da **kwan**to **a**-ee owto-**boos**es a...*

When is the first / the last bus to...?
¿Cuándo sale el primer / el último autobús para...?
***kwan**do **sa**-le el pree-**mer** / el **ool**-teemo owto-**boos** para...*

Please tell me when to get off
Por favor, ¿me dice cuándo tengo que bajarme?
*por fa**bor** me **dee**-the **kwan**do **ten**go ke ba**khar**-me*

Please let me off
¿Me deja salir, por favor?
*me **dekha** sa-**leer** por fa**bor***

This is my stop
Me bajo en esta parada
*me **ba**-kho en esta pa-**ra**ɖa*

■ YOU MAY HEAR

Este autobús no para en...
*este owto-**boos** no para en...*
This bus doesn't stop in...

Tiene que coger el...
***tye**-ne ke ko-**kher** el...*
You have to catch the...

■ METRO ■ TAXI

BOARD MEETING	LA REUNIÓN DEL CONSEJO DE ADMINISTRACIÓN
CONFERENCE ROOM	EL SALÓN DE CONFERENCIAS
MANAGING DIRECTOR	EL/LA DIRECTOR(A) GENERAL
MEETING	LA REUNIÓN
MINUTES	LAS ACTAS
SAMPLE	LA MUESTRA
TO CHAIR A MEETING	PRESIDIR
TO DRAW UP A CONTRACT	REDACTAR UN CONTRATO
TRADE FAIR	LA FERIA DE MUESTRAS
TURNOVER	EL VOLUMEN DE VENTAS

I'd like to arrange a meeting with...
Me gustaría tener una reunión con...
*me goosta-**ree**-a te-**ner** oona re-oo-**nyon** kon ...*

Are you free to meet...?   on the 4th of May at 1100
¿Está usted libre para vernos...?   el cuatro de mayo a las once
*esta oosted **lee**-bre para **ber**-nos...   el **kwa**tro de **ma**yo a las **on**-the*

for breakfast	for lunch	for dinner
para desayunar	para comer	para cenar
*para desa-yoo**nar***	*para ko**mer***	*para the-**nar***

I will confirm...	by letter	by fax
Lo confirmaré...	por escrito	por fax
*lo konfeer-ma-**re**...*	*por es**kree**-to*	*por faks*

I'm staying at Hotel...
Me quedo en el Hotel...
*me **ke**do en el o-**tel**...*

How do I get to your office?
¿Cómo se va a su oficina?
***ko**mo se ba a soo ofee-**thee**na*

Please let... know that I will be ... minutes late
Por favor, dígale a ... que voy a llegar ... minutos tarde
*por fa**bor** dee-gale a ... ke boy a lye**gar** ... mee-**noo**tos **tar**-de*

I have an appointment with...
Tengo una cita con...
*ten*go oona *thee*ta kon...

at ... o'clock
a las...
a las...

Here is my card
Aquí tiene mi tarjeta
a-*kee tye*-ne mee tar-*khe*ta

I'm delighted to meet you at last
Es un gran placer para mí conocerle(la) por fin
es oon gran pla-*ther* para mee kono-*ther*-le(la) por feen

I don't know much Spanish
No sé mucho español
no se *moo*cho espa-*nyol*

Can you speak more slowly?
¿Puede hablar más despacio?
pwe-de a-*blar* mas despa-*thyo*

I'm sorry I'm late
Siento llegar tarde
syen-to lye-*gar* tar-de

My flight was delayed
El vuelo ha venido con retraso
el *bwe*lo a be*nee*-do kon re-*tra*so

May I introduce you to...
Permítame presentarle a...
per-*mee*-tame presen-*tar*-le a...

Can I invite you to dinner?
Le(La) invito a cenar
le(la) een-*bee*to a the-*nar*

■ YOU MAY HEAR

¿Está usted citado(a)?
*esta oos*ted thee-*ta*do(a)
Do you have an appointment?

El Señor... / La Señora... no está en la oficina
el se*nyor*... / la se-*nyo*ra... no es*ta* en la ofee-*thee*na
Señor... / Señora... isn't in the office

Estará de vuelta en cinco minutos
esta-*ra* de *bwel*ta en *theen*ko mee-*noo*tos
He / She will be back in five minutes

■ FAX ■ LETTERS ■ OFFICE ■ TELEPHONE

*Local tourist offices should have **una guía de campings** with prices.*

Do you have a list of campsites with prices?
¿Tiene una guía de campings con precios?
tye-ne oona **gee**-a de **kam**peens kon **pre**thyos

Is the campsite in a sheltered place?
¿El camping, está en un sitio resguardado?
el **kam**peen es**ta** en oon **see**tyo res-gwar**da**-do

How far is the beach?
¿A qué distancia queda la playa?
a ke dees**tan**-thya **ke**da la **pla**ya

Is there a restaurant on the campsite?
¿Hay restaurante en el camping?
a-ee re-stow-**ran**te en el **kam**peen

Do you have any vacancies?
¿Tienen sitio?
tye-nen **see**tyo

Are showers... / Is hot water... / Is electricity...
¿El uso de las duchas... / ¿El agua caliente... / ¿La electricidad...
el **oo**so de las **doo**chas... / el **a**gwa kal**yen**-te... / la elek-treethee-**dad**...

...included in the price?
...va incluido en el precio?
...ba eenkloo-**ee**-do en el **pre**thyo

We'd like to stay for ... nights
Quisiéramos quedarnos ... noches
kee-**sye**-ramos ke**dar**-nos ... **no**-ches

How much is it per night...? for a tent per person
¿Cuánto cuesta por noche...? por tienda por persona
kwanto **kwes**ta por **no**-che... por **tyen**-da por per-**so**na

Can we camp here overnight? *(for tent)*
¿Podemos acampar aquí para pasar la noche?
po-**de**mos akam-**par** a-**kee** para pa**sar** la **no**-che

■ SIGHTSEEING & TOURIST OFFICE

20

*If you park in a **zona azul** you will need a parking ticket/disk.*

APARCAMIENTO	PARKING
AUTOPISTA	MOTORWAY *(signs are in blue)*
CEDA EL PASO	GIVE WAY
CENTRO CIUDAD	CITY CENTRE
CARRETERA CORTADA	ROAD CLOSED
CIRCULE POR LA DERECHA	KEEP RIGHT
CIRCUNVALACIÓN	BYPASS
CURVA PELIGROSA	DANGEROUS BEND
DIRECCIÓN ÚNICA	ONE-WAY STREET
MODERE SU VELOCIDAD	SLOW DOWN
PEAJE	TOLL
PROHIBIDO APARCAR	NO PARKING
VEHÍCULOS PESADOS	HEAVY VEHICLES
VELOCIDAD MÁXIMA	SPEED LIMIT

Can I/we park here?
¿Se puede aparcar aquí?
se **pwe**-de apar-**kar** a-**kee**

How long for?
¿Cúanto tiempo?
kwanto **tyem**po

Do I/we need a parking ticket?
¿Hace falta tique?
a-the **fal**ta **tee**-ke

We're going to....
Vamos a...
bamos a...

What is the best route?
¿Por dónde se va mejor?
por **don**-de se ba me-**khor**

Will the motorway be busy?
¿Habrá mucho tráfico en la autopista?
a-**bra moo**cho **tra**-feeko en la owto-**pee**sta

Is the pass open?
¿Está abierto el puerto?
es**ta** a-**byer**to el **pwer**to

Do I/we need snow chains?
¿Hace falta usar cadenas?
a-the **fal**ta oo**sar** ka-**de**nas

■ **BREAKDOWNS** ■ **PETROL STATION**

DRIVING LICENCE	EL CARNÉ DE CONDUCIR
FULLY COMPREHENSIVE INSURANCE	EL SEGURO A TODO RIESGO
REVERSE GEAR	LA MARCHA ATRÁS

I want to hire a car
Quería alquilar un coche
*ke-**ree**-a alkee-**lar** oon **ko**-che*

for ... days / the weekend
para ... días / el fin de semana
*para ... **dee**-as / el feen de se-**ma**na*

What are your rates...?
¿Qué tarifas tienen...?
*ke ta-**ree**fas **tye**-nen...*

per day
por día
*por **dee**-a*

per week
por semana
*por se-**ma**na*

How much is the deposit?
¿Cuánto hay que dejar de depósito?
***kwan**to **a**-ee ke de**khar** de depo-**see**to*

Is there a mileage (kilometre) charge?
¿Hay que pagar kilometraje?
***a**-ee ke pa**gar** keelo-me-**tra**khe*

How much?
¿Cuánto?
***kwan**to*

Is fully comprehensive insurance included in the price?
¿El seguro a todo riesgo, va incluido en el precio?
*el se-**goo**ro a **to**do **rye**sgo ba eenkloo-**ee**-do en el **pre**thyo*

Do I have to return the car here?
¿Hay que devolver el coche aquí mismo?
***a**-ee ke debol-**ber** el **ko**-che a-**kee mee**smo*

By what time?
¿Para qué hora?
*para ke **o**-ra*

I'd like to leave it in...
Quisiera dejarlo en...
*kee-**sye**-ra de**khar**-lo en...*

Can you show me how the controls work?
¿Me enseña cómo funcionan los mandos?
*me en-**se**nya komo foon-**thyo**-nan los **man**dos*

■ **YOU MAY HEAR**

Por favor, devuelva el coche con el depósito lleno
*por fa**bor** de-**bwel**ba el **ko**-che kon el depo-**see**to **lye**no*
Please return the car with a full tank

The ... doesn't work	**The ... don't work**
El/La ... no funciona	**Los/Las ... no funcionan**
el/la ... no foon-thyona	*los/las ... no foon-thyo-nan*

accelerator	el acelerador	*a-the-lera-dor*
battery	la bateria	*ba-teree-a*
bonnet	el capó	*kapo*
brakes	los frenos	*frenos*
choke	el stárter	*estar-ter*
clutch	el embrague	*embra-ge*
distributor	el distribuidor	*deestree-bweedor*
engine	el motor	*motor*
exhaust pipe	el tubo de escape	*toobo de eska-pe*
fuse	el fusible	*foosee-ble*
gears	las marchas	*marchas*
handbrake	el freno de mano	*freno de mano*
headlights	los faros	*faros*
ignition	el encendido	*enthen-deedo*
indicator	el intermitente	*eenter-meeten-te*
points	los platinos	*pla-teenos*
radiator	el radiador	*radya-dor*
rear lights	los pilotos	*pee-lotos*
seat belt	el cinturón de seguridad	*theen-too-ron de se-goo-ree-dad*
spare wheel	la rueda de repuesto	*rweda de repwesto*
spark plugs	las bujías	*bookhee-as*
steering	la dirección	*deerek-thyon*
steering wheel	el volante	*bolan-te*
tyre	el neumático	*ne-oo-ma-teeko*
wheel	la rueda	*rweda*
windscreen	el parabrisas	*para-breesas*
-- washer	el lavaparabrisas	*laba-para-breesas*
-- wiper	el limpiaparabrisas	*leempya-para-breesas*

■ BREAKDOWNS ■ PETROL STATION

I'd like to wish you a...
  ¡Le deseo que pase un/unas...
  *le de**se**-o ke **pa**se oon/oonas...*

I'd like to wish you a...(familiar)
  Te deseo que pases un/unas...
  *te de**se**-o ke **pa**ses oon/oonas...*

Merry Christmas!
  ¡Felices Pascuas! / ¡Feliz Navidad¡
  *fe**lee**-thes **pas**-kwas / fe**leeth** nabee-**dad**

Happy New Year!
  ¡Feliz Año Nuevo!
  *fe**leeth** a-nyo **nwe**bo*

Happy birthday!
  ¡Feliz cumpleaños!
  *fe**leeth** koom-ple-**a**-nyos*

Happy (Saint's) Name Day!
  ¡Felicidades!
  *felee-thee**da**-des*

Have a good trip!
  ¡Buen viaje!
  *bwen **bya**-khe*

Best wishes!
  ¡Felicidades!
  *felee-thee**da**-des*

Welcome!
  ¡Bienvenido(a)!
  *byen-be-**nee**do(a)*

Enjoy your meal!
  ¡Que aproveche!
  *ke a-pro**be**-che*

Thanks, and you too!
  ¡Gracias, igualmente!
  ***gra**thyas ee-gwal-**men**te*

Cheers!
  ¡Salud!
  *sa**lood***

Congratulations! (having a baby, getting married, etc.)
  ¡Enhorabuena!
  *e-nora-**bwe**na*

■ **LETTERS** ■ **MAKING FRIENDS**

PARA MAYORES DE 18 AÑOS	FOR PERSONS OVER 18
PELÍCULA DOBLADA	DUBBED FILM
SESIÓN	PERFORMANCE
VO (versión original)	ORIGINAL VERSION

What's on at the cinema?

¿Qué películas ponen?
*ke pe**lee**-koolas **po**-nen*

When does the film start?

¿A qué hora empieza (name film) ...?
*a ke **o**-ra em-**pye**tha...*

Is it dubbed or subtitled?

¿Está doblada o subtitulada?
*es**ta** do-**bla**da o soob-tee-too-**la**da*

How much are the tickets?

¿Cuánto cuestan las entradas?
***kwan**to **kwes**tan las en-**tra**das*

Two for the (time) showing

Dos para la sesión de las...
*dos para la se-**syon** de las...*

What films have you seen recently?

¿Qué películas ha visto últimamente?
*ke pe**lee**-koolas a **bees**to **ool**-teema-mente*

What is (English name of film) called in Spanish?

¿Cómo se titula ... en español?
ko**mo se tee**too**-la ... en espa-**nyol

Who is your favourite actor / actress?

Qué actor / actriz le gusta más?
*ke ak**tor** / ak-**treez** le **goo**sta mas*

■ YOU MAY HEAR

Para la sala uno / dos no quedan localidades
*para la **sala oo**no / dos no **ke**-dan lo-kalee-**da**des*
For screen 1 / 2 there are no tickets left

■ ENTERTAINMENT ■ LEISURE/INTERESTS

*Size for clothes is **la talla** Size for shoes is **el número***

women			men - suits			shoes			
sizes			**sizes**			**sizes**			
UK	EC		UK	EC		UK	EC	UK	EC
10	36		36	46		2	35	8	42
12	38		38	48		3	36	9	43
14	40		40	50		4	37	10	44
16	42		42	52		5	38	11	45
18	44		44	54		6	39		
20	46		46	56		7	41		

May I try this on?
¿Puedo probarme esto?
pwedo pro**bar**-me **es**to

Where are the changing rooms?
¿Dónde están los probadores?
don-de es**tan** los proba-**do**-res

Have you a bigger size?
¿Tiene una talla mayor?
tye-ne oona **ta**lya ma-**yor**?

Have you a smaller size?
¿Tiene una talla menor?
tye-ne oona **ta**lya me**nor**?

Do you have this...?
¿Tiene esto...?
tye-ne **es**to...

in my size
en mi talla
en mee **ta**lya

in other colours
en otros colores
en **o**-tros kolo-res

That's a shame!
¡Qué pena!
ke **pe**na

It's too short
Es demasiado corto
es dema-**sya**do **kor**to

It's too long
Es demasiado largo
es dema-**sya**do **lar**go

I'm just looking
Solo estoy mirando
solo es**toy** mee-**ran**do

I'll take it
Me lo llevo
me lo **lye**vo

■ **YOU MAY HEAR**

¿De qué talla / número?
de ke **ta**lya / **noo**-mero
What size *(clothes)* / *(shoes)*?

¿Le queda bien?
le **ke**da byen
Does it fit you?

■ **NUMBERS** ■ **PAYING** ■ **SHOPPING**

26

COTTON	EL ALGODÓN	SILK	LA SEDA
LACE	EL ENCAJE	SUEDE	EL ANTE
LEATHER	LA PIEL	WOOL	LA LANA

English	Spanish	Pronunciation
belt	el cinturón	*theentoo-**ron***
blouse	la blusa	*bloo*sa
bra	el sujetador	*soo-khe-ta**dor***
coat	el abrigo	*a-**bree**go*
dress	el vestido	*bes-**tee**do*
gloves	los guantes	***gwan**-tes*
hat	el sombrero	*som-**brero***
hat *(woollen)*	el gorro	***go**-rro*
jacket	la chaqueta	*cha-**ke**ta*
knickers	las bragas	***bra**gas*
nightdress	el camisón	*kamee-**son***
pyjamas	el pijama	*pee-**kha**ma*
raincoat	el impermeable	*eemper-me-**a**-ble*
sandals	las sandalias	*san**da**-lyas*
scarf *(silk)*	el pañuelo	*pa-**nwe**lo*
scarf *(wool)*	la bufanda	*boo-**fan**da*
shirt	la camisa	*ka-**mee**sa*
shorts	los pantalones cortos	*panta-**lo**-nes **kor**tos*
skirt	la falda	***fal**da*
slippers	las zapatillas	*thapa-**teel**yas*
socks	los calcetines	*kal-the**tee**-nes*
suit	el traje	***tra**-khe*
swimsuit	el traje de baño	***tra**-khe de **ban**yo*
tie	la corbata	*kor-**ba**ta*
tights	las medias	***me**dyas*
tracksuit	el chándal	***chan**dal*
trousers	los pantalones	*panta-**lo**-nes*
t-shirt	la camiseta	*kamee-**se**ta*
underpants	los calzoncillos	*kalthon-**theel**yos*
zip	la cremallera	*krema-**lye**ra*

27

Two key words for describing colours in Spanish are:
claro light   **oscuro** dark

black	negro	**ne**gro
blue	azul	a-**thool**
navy blue	azul marino	a-**thool** ma-**ree**no
brown	marrón	ma-**rron**
cream	crema	**kre**ma
crimson	rojo vivo	**ro**kho **bee**-bo
gold	dorado	do-**ra**do
green	verde	**ber**-de
grey	gris	grees
orange	color naranja	ko**lor** na-**ran**kha
pink	rosa	**ro**sa
shocking pink	fucsia	**fook**-sya
purple	morado	mo-**ra**do
red	rojo	**ro**kho
silver	plateado	pla-te-**a**do
turquoise	azul turquesa	a-**thool** toor **ke**sa
white	blanco	**blan**ko
yellow	amarillo	ama-**ree**lyo

■ SHAPE

big	grande	**gran**-de
fat	gordo(a)	**gor**do(a)
flat	llano(a)	**lya**no(a)
long	largo(a)	**lar**go(a)
narrow	estrecho(a)	es-**tre**cho(a)
round	redondo(a)	re**don**-do(a)
small	pequeño(a)	pe-**ke**nyo(a)
square	cuadrado(a)	kwa-**dra**do(a)
tall	alto(a)	**al**to(a)
thick	grueso(a)	**grwe**so(a)
thin	delgado(a)	del-**ga**do(a)
tiny	pequeñito(a)	pe-ke-**nyee**to(a)
wide	ancho(a)	**an**cho(a)

This doesn't work
Esto no funciona
esto no foon-thyona

The ... doesn't work
El/La ... no funciona
el/la ... no foon-thyona

The ... don't work
Los/Las ... no funcionan
los/las ... no foon-thyo-nan

light
la luz
la looth

heating
la calefacción
la ka-lefak-thyon

air conditioning
el aire acondicionado
el a-ee-re a-kondee-thyo-nado

There's a problem with the room
La habitación tiene un problema
la abeeta-thyon tye-ne oon pro-blema

It's noisy
Hay mucho ruido
a-ee moocho rwee-do

It's too hot (room)
Hace demasiado calor
a-the dema-syado kalor

It's too cold (room)
Hace demasiado frío
a-the dema-syado free-o

It's too hot / too cold (food)
Está muy caliente / muy frío
esta mwee kalyen-te / mwee free-o

The meat is cold
La carne está fría
la kar-ne esta free-a

This isn't what I ordered
Esto no es lo que he pedido yo
esto no es lo ke he pe-deedo yo

To whom should I complain?
¿Para una queja, con quién tengo que hablar?
para oona ke-kha kon kyen tengo ke a-blar

It's faulty
Tiene un defecto
tye-ne oon de-fekto

I want a refund
Quiero devolverlo
kyero de-bol-berlo

The goods were damaged in transit
La mercancía se estropeó durante el trayecto
la merkan-thee-a se es-trope-o doo-rante el tra-yekto

■ PROBLEMS ■ REPAIRS ■ ROOM SERVICE

COMPUTERS ――――――――――― ENGLISH-SPANISH

COMPUTER	EL ORDENADOR / EL COMPUTADOR
DATABASE	LA BASE DE DATOS
FILE	EL FICHERO
FLOPPY DISK	EL DISQUETE
HARD DISK	EL DISCO DURO
KEYBOARD	EL TECLADO
PRINT-OUT	LA IMPRESIÓN
SCREEN	LA PANTALLA

What computer do you use?
¿Qué ordenador usa?
*ke ordena-**dor** oo*sa

Is it IBM compatible?
¿Es compatible con IBM?
*es kompa-**tee**-ble kon **ee**-be-eme*

Do you have E-mail?
¿Tiene usted correo electrónico?
***tye**-ne oos*ted *ko-**rre**-o elek-**tro**nee-ko*

What is your address?
¿Cuál es su dirección?
*kwal es soo deerek-**thyon***

Do you have a database?
¿Tiene base de datos?
***tye**-ne **ba**se de **da**-tos*

How often do you update it?
¿Cada cuánto tiempo lo actualizar?
***ka**da **kwan**to **tyem**po lo ak-twa-**lee**than*

Can you send it on a floppy disk?
¿Puede mandarlo en disquete?
*pwe-de man-**dar**lo en dees-**ke**te*

What word processing package do you use?
¿Qué procesador de textos usa?
*ke pro-thesa-**dor** de **teks**tos oo*sa

How much memory does the computer have?
¿Cuánta memoria RAM tiene el computador?
kwan**ta me-**mo**rya ram **tye**-ne el kompoo-ta**dor

■ OFFICE

*With the single European Market, EC citizens are subject only to highly selective spot checks and they can go through the blue customs channel (unless they have goods to declare). There is no restriction, either by quantity or value, on goods purchased by travellers in another EC country provided they are **for their own personal use** (guidelines have been published). If you are unsure of certain items, check with the customs officials as to whether payment of duty is required.*

CONTROL DE PASAPORTES	PASSPORT CONTROL
CEE	EEC
DOCUMENTO NACIONAL DE IDENTIDAD	NATIONAL IDENTITY DOCUMENT
ADUANA	CUSTOMS

Do I have to pay duty on this?
¿Hay que pagar derechos de aduana por esto?
*a-ee ke pa**gar** de-**re**chos de a-**dwa**na por **es**to*

I bought this as a gift
He comprado esto para regalar
*e kom**pra**-do **es**to para rega-**lar***

It is for my own personal use
Es para uso personal
*es para **oo**so perso-**nal***

We are on our way to... *(if in transit through a country)*
Estamos aquí de paso. Vamos a...
*es**ta**-mos a-**kee** de **pa**so **ba**mos a...*

The children are on this passport
Los niños están en este pasaporte
*los **nee**nyos es**tan** en **es**te pasa-**por**-te*

days

MONDAY	LUNES
TUESDAY	MARTES
WEDNESDAY	MIÉRCOLES
THURSDAY	JUEVES
FRIDAY	VIERNES
SATURDAY	SÁBADO
SUNDAY	DOMINGO

seasons

SPRING	LA PRIMAVERA
SUMMER	EL VERANO
AUTUMN	EL OTOÑO
WINTER	EL INVIERNO

months

JANUARY	ENERO
FEBRUARY	FEBRERO
MARCH	MARZO
APRIL	ABRIL
MAY	MAYO
JUNE	JUNIO
JULY	JULIO
AUGUST	AGOSTO
SEPTEMBER	SEPTIEMBRE
OCTOBER	OCTUBRE
NOVEMBER	NOVIEMBRE
DECEMBER	DICIEMBRE

What is today's date?
¿Qué fecha es hoy?
*ke **fe**cha es oy*

What day is it today?
¿Qué día es hoy?
*ke **dee**-a es oy*

It's the 5th of March 1993
Es el cinco de marzo de mil novecientos noventa y tres
*es el **theen**ko de **mar**tho de meel no-be-**thyen**tos no-**ben**ta ee tres*

on Saturday
el sábado
*el **sa**-bado*

on Saturdays
los sábados
*los **sa**-bados*

every Saturday
todos los sábados
***to**dos los **sa**-bados*

this Saturday
este sábado
***es**te **sa**-bado*

next Saturday
el sábado que viene
*el **sa**-bado ke **bye**-ne*

last Saturday
el sábado pasado
*el **sa**-bado pa-**sa**do*

in June
en junio
*en **khoo**nyo*

at the beginning of June
a primeros de junio
*a pree-**me**ros de **khoo**nyo*

at the end of June
a finales de junio
*a fee**na**-les de **khoo**nyo*

before summer
antes del verano
***an**-tes del be-**ra**no*

during the summer
por el verano
*por el be-**ra**no*

after summer
después del verano
*des-**pwes** del be-**ra**no*

■ NUMBERS

FILLING	EL EMPASTE
CROWN	LA FUNDA
DENTURES	LA DENTADURA POSTIZA
A TEMPORARY REPAIR	UN ARREGLO PROVISIONAL

I need a dentist
Necesito un dentista
ne-the-**see**to oon den-**tee**sta

He / She has toothache
Tiene dolor de muelas
tye-ne do**lor** de **mwe**-las

Can you do a temporary filling?
¿Puede hacer un empaste provisional?
pwe-de a-**ther** oon em-**pas**te pro boosyo-**nal**

It hurts (me)
Me duele
me **dwe**-le

Can you give me something for the pain?
¿Puede darme algo para el dolor?
pwe-de **dar**-me **al**go para el do**lor**

I think I have an abscess
Creo que tengo un absceso
kre-o ke **ten**go oon abs-**the**so

Can you repair my dentures?
¿Puede arreglarme la dentadura postiza?
pwe-de a-rre-**glar**me la denta-**doo**ra pos-**tee**tha

Do I have to pay?
¿Tengo que pagar?
tengo ke pa**gar**

How much will it be?
¿Cuánto me va a costar?
kwanto me ba a kos**tar**

I need a receipt for my insurance
Necesito un recibo para el seguro
ne-the-**see**to oon re-**thee**bo para el se-**goo**ro

■ YOU MAY HEAR

Hay que sacarla
a-ee ke sa**kar**-la
It has to come out

Voy a ponerle una inyección
boy a po**ner**le oona eenyek-**thyon**
I'm going to give you an injection

33

OPPOSITE (TO)	ENFRENTE (DE)	en-**fren**-te (de)
NEXT TO	AL LADO DE	al **la**do de
NEAR TO	CERCA DE	**ther**ka de
TRAFFIC LIGHTS	EL SEMÁFORO	se**ma**-foro
AT THE CORNER	EN LA ESQUINA	en la es-**kee**na

Excuse me, sir / madam!
¡Oiga, señor / señora!
oyga sen**yor** / se-**nyo**ra

How do I/we get to...?
¿Cómo se va a...?
komo se ba a...

to the station
a la estación
a la esta-**thyon**

to the Prado
al museo del Prado
al moo-**se**-o del **pra**do

to Sóller
a Sóller
a **so**-lyer

We're looking for...
Estamos buscando...
es-**ta**mos boos-**kan**do...

Is it far?
¿Está lejos?
esta **le**khos

Can I/we walk there?
¿Se puede ir andando?
se **pwe**-de eer an-**dan**do

We're lost
Nos hemos perdido
nos **e**-mos per-**dee**do

Is this the right way to...?
¿Se va por aquí a...?
se ba por a-**kee** a...

How do I/we get onto the motorway?
¿Por dónde se entra en la autopista?
por **don**-de se **en**tra en lo **ow**to-**pee**sta

Can you show me where it is on the map?
¿Puede indicarme dónde está en el mapa?
pwe-de een-dee**kar**-me **don**-de esta en el **ma**pa

■ **YOU MAY HEAR**

Después de pasar el puente
des-**pwes** de pa**sar** el **pwen**-te
After passing the bridge

Gire a la izquierda / derecha
kheere a la eeth-**kyer**da / de-**re**cha
Turn left / right

Siga todo recto hasta llegar a...
seega **to**do **rek**to asta lye**gar** a...
Keep straight on until you get to...

■ BASICS ■ MAPS, GUIDES & NEWSPAPERS

What facilities do you have for disabled people?
¿Qué instalaciones tienen para minusválidos?
*ke eensta-la**thyo**-nes **tye**-nen para meenoos-**ba**lee-dos*

Are there any toilets for the disabled?
¿Hay aseos especiales para minusválidos?
*a-ee a-**se**os es-pe**thya**-les para meenoos-**ba**lee-dos*

Do you have any bedrooms on the ground floor?
¿Tienen alguna habitación en la planta baja?
tye-nen al-**goo**na abeeta-**thyon** en la **plan**ta ba**kha*

Is there a lift?
¿Hay ascensor?
*a-ee as-then**sor***

Where is the lift?
¿Dónde está el ascensor?
don-de esta el as-then**sor***

Are there any ramps?
¿Hay rampas?
*a-ee **ram**pas*

Is there an induction loop?
¿Hay audífonos?
*a-ee ow-**dee**-fonos*

How many stairs are there?
¿Cuántas escaleras hay?
kwantas eska-**le**ras a-ee*

How wide is the entrance door?
¿Cómo es de ancha la puerta de entrada?
komo es de **an**cha la **pwer**ta de en-**tra**da*

Where is the wheelchair-accessible entrance?
¿Dónde está el acceso para sillas de ruedas?
don-de esta el ak**the**-so para **see**lyas de **rwe**das*

Is there a reduction for handicapped people?
¿Hacen descuento a los minusválidos?
*a-then des-**kwen**to a los meenoos-**ba**lee-dos*

Is there somewhere I can sit down?
¿Hay algún sitio donde pueda sentarme?
*a-ee al-**goon** **see**tyo **don**-de **pwe**da sen**tar**me*

■ ACCOMMODATION ■ HOTEL

35

HOSPITAL	HOSPITAL
URGENCIAS	CASUALTY DEPARTMENT
HORAS DE CONSULTA	SURGERY HOURS

I need a doctor
Necesito un médico
ne-the-**see**-to oon **me**-deeko

I have a pain here (point)
Me duele aquí
me **dwe**-le a-**kee**

My son / daughter is ill
Mi hijo / hija está enfermo(a)
mee **ee**kho / **ee**kha esta enfermo(a)

He / She has a temperature
Tiene fiebre
tye-ne **fye**-bre

I'm diabetic
Soy diabético(a)
soy dee-a-**be**teeko(a)

I'm pregnant
Estoy embarazada
estoy emba-ra**tha**-da

I'm on the pill
Tomo la píldora
tomo la **peel**-dora

I'm allergic to penicillin
Soy alérgico(a) a la penicilina
soy a-**ler**khee-ko(a) a la penee-thee**lee**-na

My blood group is...
Mi grupo sanguíneo es...
mee **groo**po sangee-ne-o es...

Will he / she have to go to hospital?
¿Tendrá que ir al hospital?
ten-**dra** ke eer al ospee-**tal**

Will I have to pay?
¿Tengo que pagar?
tengo ke pa**gar**

How much will it cost?
¿Cuánto me va a costar?
kwanto me ba a kost**ar**

I need a receipt for the insurance
Necesito un recibo para el seguro
ne-the-**see**to oon re-**thee**bo para el se-**goo**ro

■ **YOU MAY HEAR**

Tiene que ingresar
tye-ne ke een-gre**sar**
You will have to be admitted to hospital

No es grave
no es **gra**ve
It's not serious

■ BODY ■ EMERGENCIES ■ PHARMACY

If you want a strong black coffee ask for **un café solo**. For a white coffee ask for **un café con leche**.
A refreshing drink in summer is **un granizado**, an iced fresh fruit drink either **de limón** (lemon) or **de naranja** (orange).

---

a coffee	**a lager**	**a dry sherry**	**...please**
un café	una cerveza	un fino	...por favor
oon ka-**fe**	oona ther-**be**tha	oɴ **fee**no	...por fa**bor**

a tea...	**with milk**	**with lemon**	**no sugar**
un té...	con leche	con limón	sin azúcar
oon te...	kon **le**-che	kon lee-**mon**	seen a-**thoo**kar

for two	**for me**	**for him / her**	**for us**
para dos	para mí	para él / ella	para nosotros
para dos	para mee	para el / **e**-lya	para no-**so**tros

with ice, please
con hielo, por favor
kon **ye**lo por fa**bor**

A bottle of mineral water	**sparkling**	**still**
Una botella de agua mineral	con gas	sin gas
oona bo-**te**lya de **a**gwa mee-ne**ral**	kon gas	sin gas

Would you like a drink?	**What will you have?**
¿Le apetece tomar algo?	¿Qué toma?
le a-pe**te**-the to**mar al**go	ke **to**ma

I'm very thirsty	**It's my round!**
Tengo mucha sed	¡Esta ronda me toca a mí!
tengo **moo**cha sed	**es**ta **ron**da me **to**ka a mee

■ OTHER DRINKS TO TRY

un café con hielo iced coffee
un chocolate rich-tasting hot chocolate, often served with **churros**
una horchata refreshing tiger nut milk
un zumo juice: **de melocotón** peach, **de albaricoque** apricot
un anís aniseed apéritif

■ EATING OUT ■ WINES & SPIRITS

In Spain, everything happens very late – including eating. Lunch is usually between 1 and 3 pm and dinner between 8.30 and 11 pm. For those who are vegetarian, or who prefer vegetarian dishes, turn to the VEGETARIAN topic for further phrases.

Where can I/we have a snack?
¿Dónde se puede comer algo?
*don-de se **pwe**-de ko**mer al**go*

not too expensive
que no sea demasiado caro
*ke no **se**-a dema-**sya**do **ka**ro*

Can you recommend a good local restaurant?
¿Puede recomendarnos algún buen restaurante de aquí?
pwe**-de reko-men**dar**-nos al-**goon** bwen restow-**ran**-te de a-**kee

I'd like to book a table for ... people
Quisiera reservar una mesa para ... personas
*kee-**sye**-ra reser-**bar** oona **me**sa para ... per-**so**nas*

for tonight...
para esta noche...
*para **es**ta **no**-che...*

for tomorrow night...
para mañana por la noche...
*para ma-**nya**na por la **no**-che...*

at 9pm
a las nueve
*a las **nwe**-be*

The menu, please
La carta, por favor
*la **kar**ta por fa**bor***

What is the dish of the day?
¿Cuál es el plato del día?
*kwal es el **pla**to del **dee**-a*

Do you have...?
¿Tienen...?
***tye**-nen...*

a set-price menu
menú del día
*me**noo** del **dee**-a*

a children's menu
menú para niños
*me**noo** para **nee**nyos*

Can you recommend a local dish?
¿Puede recomendarnos algún plato típico de aquí?
pwe**-de reko-men**dar**-nos al-**goon pla**to **tee**-peeko de a-**kee

What is in this?
¿Este plato, que lleva?
***es**te **pla**to ke **lye**ba*

I'll have this
Voy a tomar esto
*boy a to**mar es**to*

Excuse me!
¡Oiga, por favor!
oy**ga por fa**bor

Please bring...
¿Nos trae...?
*nos **tra**-e...*

more bread
más pan
mas pan

more water
más agua
*mas **a**gwa*

another bottle
otra botella
***o**-tra bo-**te**lya*

the bill
la cuenta
*la **kwen**ta*

Is service included?
¿Está incluido el servicio?
*esta eenkloo-**ee**do el ser-**bee**thyo*

■ EATING PLACES

Bar *serves drinks, coffee, light breakfasts and often* **tapas** *or* **pinchos** *(small snacks) and* **bocadillos** *(sandwiches)*

Cafetería *serves* **platos combinados** *(i.e. main set dishes),* **sandwiches** *(usually toasted), and* **pasteles** *(cakes)*

Mesón *traditional-style tavern*

Restaurante *restaurant*

■ TAPAS	**APPETIZERS/SNACKS**
aceitunas	*olives*
boquerones	*fresh anchovies*
calamares	*fried squid rings*
champiñones	*mushrooms*
chorizo	*spicy red salami-type sausage*
gambas	*prawns*
jamón serrano	*cured ham*
pinchos morunos	*pork kebabs*
tortilla	*sliced omelette with potato*

■ ENTREMESES	**STARTER/FIRST COURSE**
ensalada de la casa	*lettuce, tomatoes, onion*
espárragos	*asparagus*
gazpacho	*cold tomato and vegetable soup*
jamón serrano	*cured ham*
sopa (de pescado)	*soup (fish)*

■ CARNES	**MEAT DISHES**
albóndigas	*meatballs in sauce*
bistec	*steak*
cabrito	*kid*
callos	*tripe*
cerdo	*pork*
cocido	*meat stew with chickpeas*
conejo	*rabbit*
cordero	*lamb*

cordoniz	quail
chuletas	chops
chuletón	large chop
entrecot	entrecôte steak
escalope de ternera	veal escalope
estofado de cordero	lamb stew
filete	fillet steak
lechazo	young lamb
liebre	hare
mollejas	sweetbreads
pato	duck
pavo asado	roast turkey
pechuga de pollo	chicken breast
perdiz	partridge
pollo	chicken
riñones al jerez	kidneys in a sherry sauce
solomillo	sirloin steak

■ PESCADOS — **FISH AND SEAFOOD**

almejas	clams
angulas	baby eel
atún	tuna
bacalao	dried salt cod
bonito	type of tunny fish
calamares en su tinta	squid cooked in its own ink
gambas a la plancha	grilled prawns
langosta	lobster
langostinos	king prawns
lenguado	sole
lubina	bass
mejillones	mussels
merluza	hake
mero	grouper
platija	plaice

pez espada	*swordfish*
rape	*monkfish*
salmonetes	*red mullet*
sardinas	*sardines*
trucha	*trout*
zarzuela de mariscos	*assorted grilled seafood*

■ VERDURAS — VEGETABLES

berenjenas	*aubergines*
cebollas	*onions*
espinacas gratinadas	*spinach au gratin*
habas	*broad beans*
judías verdes	*French beans*
menestra de verduras	*vegetables (cooked with ham)*
patatas fritas	*chips*
pimientos rellenos	*stuffed peppers*
tomates	*tomatoes*

■ POSTRES — DESSERTS

What desserts are there?
¿Qué hay de postre?
ke **a**-ee de **pos**-tre

tarta helada	*ice-cream cake dessert*
flan	*type of crème caramel*
copas de helado	*selection of ice creams*
fruta del tiempo	*fruit in season*

What cheeses do you have?
¿Qué quesos tienen?
ke **ke**sos **tye**-nen

queso manchego	*hard cheese from La Mancha*
queso de Roncal	*hard smoked sheep's cheese*
queso de Mahón	*strong hard cheese from Menorca*
queso de cabrales	*strong blue cheese from Asturias*

■ DRINKING ■ VEGETARIAN ■ WINES & SPIRITS

POLICÍA	POLICE
AMBULANCIA	AMBULANCE
BOMBEROS	FIRE BRIGADE
URGENCIAS	CASUALTY DEPARTMENT

Help!
¡Socorro!
so-korro

Fire!
¡Fuego!
fwego

Can you help me?
¿Me puede ayudar?
me pwe-de ayoo-dar

There's been an accident!
¡Ha habido un accidente!
a abee-do oon akthee-dente

Someone is injured
Hay un herido
a-ee oon e-reedo

Someone has been knocked down by a car
Han atropellado a una persona
an a-trope-lyado a oona per-sona

Call...
Llame a...
lya-me a...

the police
la policía
la polee-thee-a

an ambulance
una ambulancia
oona amboo-lanthya

please
por favor
por fabor

Where is the police station?
¿Dónde está la comisaría?
don-de esta la komee-saree-a

I want to report a theft
Quiero denunciar un robo
kyero de-noon-thyar oon robo

I've been robbed / attacked
Me han robado / agredido
me an ro-bado / agre-deedo

Someone's stolen my...
Me han robado...
me an ro-bado...

bag
el bolso
el bolso

traveller's cheques
los cheques de viaje
los che-kes de bya-khe

My car has been broken into
Me han entrado en el coche
me an en-trado en el ko-che

My car has been stolen
Me han robado el coche
me an ro-bado el ko-che

I've been raped
Me han violado
me an byo-lado

I want to speak to a policewoman
Quiero hablar con una mujer policía
kyero a-blar kon oona moo-kher pulee-thee-a

I need to make an urgent telephone call
Necesito hacer una llamada urgente
ne-the-seeto a-ther oona lya-mada oor-khen-te

I need a report for my insurance
Necesito un informe para el seguro
ne-the-seeto oon een-forme para el se-gooro

I didn't know the speed limit
No sabía cual era el límite de velocidad
no sa-bee-a kwal e-ra el lee-meete de belo-thee-dad

How much is the fine?
¿De cuánto es la multa?
de kwanto es la moolta

Where do I pay it?
¿Dónde la pago?
don-de la pago

Do I have to pay it straightaway?
¿Tengo que pagarla inmediatamente?
tengo ke pagar-la een-medyata-men-te

I'm very sorry
Lo siento mucho
lo syento moocho

■ **YOU MAY HEAR**

Se ha saltado el semáforo en rojo
se a sal-tado el sema-foro en rokho
You went through a red light

■ BODY ■ DOCTOR

43

*In large cities you can often find **La Guía del Ocio**, a magazine listing events and entertainment. Newspapers usually carry a page called **Agenda cultural** with local events.*

What is there to do in the evenings?
  ¿Qué se puede hacer por las noches?
  *ke se **pwe**-de a-**ther** por las **no**-ches*

Do you know what events are on this week?
  ¿Sabe qué actividades culturales hay esta semana?
  *sabe ke aktee-bee**da**-des kool-too**ra**-les a-ee esta se-**ma**na*

Is there anything for children?
  ¿Hay algo para niños?
  *a-ee **al**go para **nee**nyos*

Where can I/we get tickets...?   **for tonight**
  ¿Dónde se sacan las entradas...?   para esta noche
  don-de se sakan las en-tra-das...   *para esta no-che*

for the show   **for the football match**
  para la función   para el partido de fútbol
  para la foon-thyon   *para el par-tee-do de foot-bol*

I'd like ... tickets   **...adults**   **...children**
  Quisiera ... entradas   ...para mayores   ...para niños
  kee-sye-ra ... en-tra-das   *...para ma-yo-res* *...para neenyos*

Where can we go dancing?   **What time does it open?**
  ¿Adónde podemos ir a bailar?   ¿A qué hora abren?
  a-don-de pode-mos eer a ba-eelar   *a ke o-ra a-bren*

How much is it to get in?
  ¿Cuánto cuesta entrar?
  kwanto kwesta en-trar

■ **YOU MAY HEAR**

La entrada cuesta ... pesetas con derecho a consumición
  la en-tra-da kwesta ... pese-tas kon de-recho a konsoo-meethyon
  It costs ... pesetas to get in including a free drink

■ **CINEMA** ■ **SIGHTSEEING & TOURIST OFFICE** ■ **THEATRE**

*To fax Spain from the UK, the code is **00 34** followed by the Spanish area code, e.g. Madrid **1**, Bilbao **4**, and the fax number.*

ADDRESSING A FAX	
FROM	DE
FOR THE ATTENTION OF	A LA ATENCIÓN DE
DATE	FECHA
RE:	CON REFERENCIA A
THIS DOCUMENT CONTAINS ... PAGES INCLUDING THIS	ESTE DOCUMENTO CONTIENE ... PÁGINAS, ESTA INCLUSIVE

Do you have a fax?
¿Tiene fax?
__tye__-ne faks

I want to send a fax
Quería mandar un fax
ke-__ree__-a man__dar__ oon faks

What is your fax number?
¿Cuál es su número de fax?
kwal es soo __noo__-mero de faks

I am having trouble getting through to your fax
No consigo enviarle el fax
no kon-__see__go en-__byar__-le el faks

Please resend your fax
Por favor, vuélvame a mandar su fax
por fa__bor__ __bwel__ba-me a man__dar__ soo faks

I can't read it
No se entiende
no se en-__tyen__de

The fax is constantly engaged
El fax está ocupado constantemente
el faks es__ta__ okoo-__pa__do konstan-__te__-mente

Can I send a fax from here?
¿Puedo mandar un fax desde aquí?
__pwe__do man__dar__ oon faks __des__de a-__kee__

■ **LETTERS** ■ **TELEPHONE**

biscuits	las galletas	ga-**lye**tas
bread	el pan	pan
bread (brown)	el pan integral	pan een-te**gral**
bread roll	el panecillo	pa-ne-**thee**lyo
butter	la mantequilla	man-te-**kee**-lya
cereal	los cereales	the-re-**a**-les
cheese	el queso	**ke**so
chicken	el pollo	**po**lyo
coffee (instant)	el café (instantáneo)	ka-**fe** (eenstan-**tan**e-o)
cream	la nata	**na**ta
crisps	las patatas fritas	pa-**ta**tas **free**tas
eggs	los huevos	**we**bos
flour	la harina	a-**ree**na
ham (cooked)	el jamón de York	kha**mon** de york
ham (cured)	el jamón serrano	kha**mon** se-**rra**no
herbal tea	la infusión	een-foo-**syon**
honey	la miel	myel
jam	la mermelada	mer-me**la**-da
margarine	la margarina	marga-**ree**na
marmalade	la mermelada de naranja	mer-me**la**-da de na-**ran**kha
milk	la leche	**le**-che
mustard	la mostaza	mos-**ta**tha
olive oil	el aceite de oliva	a-**the**-ee-te de o-**lee**ba
orange juice	el zumo de naranja	**thoo**mo de na-**ran**kha
pepper	la pimienta	pee-**myen**ta
rice	el arroz	a-**rroth**
salt	la sal	sal
stock cube	el cubito de caldo	koo-**bee**to de **kal**do
sugar	el azúcar	a-**thoo**kar
tea	el té	te
tin of tomatoes	la lata de tomates	**la**ta de to-**ma**tes
vinegar	el vinagre	bee**na**-gre
yoghurt	el yogur	yo**goor**

■ FRUIT

apples	las manzanas	man-**tha**nas
apricots	los albaricoques	alba-reeko-kes
bananas	los plátanos	**pla**-tanos
cherries	las cerezas	the-**re**thas
grapefruit	el pomelo	po-**me**lo
grapes	las uvas	**oo**-bas
lemon	el limón	lee-**mon**
melon	el melón	me-**lon**
nectarines	las nectarinas	nekta-**ree**nas
oranges	las naranjas	na-**ran**khas
peaches	los melocotones	melo-koto-nes
pears	las peras	**pe**ras
pineapple	la piña	**pee**nya
plums	las ciruelas	thee-**rwe**las
raspberries	las frambuesas	fram-**bwe**sas
strawberries	las fresas	**fre**sas
watermelon	la sandía	san-**dee**-a

■ VEGETABLES

asparagus	los espárragos	es**pa**-rragos
carrots	las zanahorias	thana-**o**-ryas
cauliflower	la coliflor	kolee-**flor**
courgettes	los calabacines	kala-ba**thee**-nes
French beans	las judías verdes	**khoo**dee-as **ber**-des
garlic	el ajo	**a**-kho
leeks	los puerros	**pwe**rros
lettuce	la lechuga	le-**choo**ga
mushrooms	los champiñones	champee-**nyo**-nes
onions	las cebollas	the-**bol**yas
peas	los guisantes	gee**san**-tes
peppers	los pimientos	pee-**myen**tos
potatoes	las patatas	pa-**ta**tas
spinach	las espinacas	espee-**na**kas
tomatoes	los tomates	toma-tes

You will often find the Spanish quite formal in their greetings, shaking hands both on meeting and parting. Frequent greetings include hola, buenos días, senor or hola, buenas tardes, señora If you are saying good night and leaving you would say adiós, buenas noches

Hello!
¡Hola!
o-la

Goodbye!
¡Adiós!
a-*dyos*

Good morning *(until after lunch)*
Buenos días
*bwe*nos *dee*-as

Good afternoon / Good evening *(until dusk)*
Buenas tardes
*bwe*nas *tar*-des

Good evening / Good night *(after dark)*
Buenas noches
*bwe*nas *no*-ches

Pleased to meet you
Encantado(a)
enkan-*ta*do(a)

It's a pleasure
Mucho gusto
*moo*cho *goo*sto

How are you?
¿Cómo está?
*ko*mo esta

Fine, thanks
Bien, gracias
byen gra*thyas*

And you?
¿Y usted?
ee oos*ted*

How are things?
¿Qué tal?
ke tal

See you tomorrow
Hasta mañana
*a*sta ma-*nya*na

See you later
Hasta luego
*a*sta *lwe*-go

Until we meet again
Hasta la vista
*a*sta la *bee*sta

■ BASICS ■ MAKING FRIENDS

These phrases are intended for use at the hotel desk. More details about rooms can be found in the ACCOMMODATION topic.

Do you have a room for tonight?
¿Tiene una habitación para esta noche?
*tye-ne oona abee-ta**thyon** para esta **no**-che*

I booked a room...
Tengo una habitación reservada...
*tengo oona abee-ta**thyon** reser-ba*da...

in the name of...
a nombre de...
*a **nom**-bre de...*

I'd like to see the room
Quisiera ver la habitación
*kee-**sye**-ra ber la abee-ta**thyon***

Have you anything else?
¿No tiene otra cosa?
no tye-ne otra kosa

Where can I park the car?
¿Dónde puedo aparcar el coche?
***don**-de **pwe**do apar-**kar** el **ko**-che*

What time is...?
¿A qué hora es...?
*a ke **o**-ra es...*

dinner
la cena
*la **the**na*

breakfast
el desayuno
*el desa-**yoo**no*

We'll be back late tonight
Esta noche vamos a volver tarde
*esta **no**-che bamos a bol-**ber** tarde*

Do you lock the door?
¿Cierran ustedes la puerta?
***thye**-rran ooste-des la **pwer**ta*

The key for room number...
¿Me da la llave de la...?
*me da la **lya**-be de la...*

Are there any messages for me?
¿Hay algún mensaje para mí?
*a-ee al-**goon** men**sa**-khe para mee*

I'm leaving tomorrow
Me voy mañana
*me boy ma-**nya**na*

Please prepare the bill
¿Me hace la cuenta, por favor?
*me **a**-the la **kwen**ta por fa**bor***

Can I leave my luggage until...?
¿Puedo dejar el equipaje hasta...?
***pwe**do de**khar** el ekee-**pa**khe **a**sta...*

■ **ACCOMMODATION** ■ **ROOM SERVICE**

*The Single European Market allows goods within the EC to travel freely. Businesses which supply goods to VAT-registered EC companies are required to complete a Sales List which accompanies the goods. The Spanish VAT registration code (CIF – **Código de Identificación Fiscal**) is **ES** followed by the Spanish company's 9-digit number. VAT is paid at the rate of the destination country.*

What is your fiscal code number *(VAT number)***?**
¿Cuál es su CIF?
*kwal es soo the ee **e**-fe*

Our VAT number is... *(GB followed by number)*
Nuestro número de IVA es el...
***nwe**stro **noo**-mero de **ee**-ba es el...*

The goods should be delivered to...
La mercancía debe ser entregada a *(person)..* / en *(place)..*
*la merkan-**thee**-a debe ser en-tre**ga**-da a... / en...*

The consignment must be accompanied by a pro forma invoice
El envío debe ir acompañado de una factura pro forma
*el en-**byo** debe eer a-kom-pan**ya**-do de oona fak-**too**ra pro **for**ma*

How long will it take to deliver?
¿Cuánto tiempo tardará en ser entregado?
***kwan**to **tyem**po tar-da**ra** en ser en-tre**ga**-do*

Delivery will take ... days / weeks
La mercancía será entregada dentro de ... días / semanas
*la merkan-**thee**-a se**ra** en-tre**ga**-da **den**tro de ... **dee**-as / se-ma**na**s*

Please fax a copy of the pro forma invoice
Por favor, mande por fax una copia de la factura pro forma
*por fa**bor man**de por faks oona **ko**pya de la fak-**too**ra pro **s**ma*

Please confirm safe delivery of the goods
Por favor, confirmen si ha llegado la mercancía en buenas condiciones   *por fa**bor** kon**feer**-men see a lye**ga**-do la merkan-**thee**-a en **bwe**nas kondee-**thyo**-nes*

■ **NUMBERS** ■ **OFFICE**

DRY-CLEANER'S	LA TINTORERÍA / LA LIMPIEZA EN SECO
LAUNDERETTE	LA LAVANDERÍA AUTOMÁTICA
WASHING POWDER	EL DETERGENTE EN POLVO

Where can I do some washing?
¿Dónde puedo lavar un poco de ropa?
don-de pwedo labar oon poko de ropa

Do you have a laundry service?
¿Tienen servicio de lavandería?
tye-nen ser-beethyo de laban-deree-a

When will my things be ready?
¿Para cuándo estarán mis cosas?
para kwando esta-ran mees kosas

Is there a launderette near here?
¿Hay alguna lavandería automática por aquí cerca?
a-ee al-goona laban-deree-a owto-matee-ka por a-kee therka

When does it open?	**When does it close?**
¿Cuándo abren?	¿Cuándo cierran?
kwando a-bren	*kwando thye-rran*

What coins do I need?
¿Qué monedas hay que usar?
ke mone-das a-ee ke oosar

Is there somewhere to dry clothes?
¿Hay algún sitio para secar la ropa?
a-ee al-goon seetyo para sekar la ropa

Can you iron these clothes?
¿Pueden plancharme esta ropa?
pwe-den planchar-me esta ropa

Can I borrow an iron?
¿Me pueden dejar una plancha?
me pwe-den dekhar oona plancha

■ **ROOM SERVICE**

Where can I/we go...?   fishing   riding
¿Adónde se puede ir a...?   pescar   montar a caballo
*a-**don**-de se **pwe**-de eer a...*   *pes**kar***   *mon**tar** a ka-**bal**yo*

Are there any good beaches near here?
¿Hay alguna playa buena cerca de aquí?
*a-ee al-**goo**na **pla**ya **bwe**na **ther**ka de a-**kee***

Is there a swimming pool?
¿Hay piscina?
*a-ee pees-**thee**na*

Where can I/we hire mountain bikes?
¿Dónde alquilan bicis de montaña?
***don**-de al**kee**-lan **bee**thees de mon-**ta**nya*

Do you have cycling helmets?
¿Tienen cascos de ciclista?
***tye**-nen **kas**kos de thee-**klee**sta*

How much is it...?   **per hour**   **per day**
¿Cuánto cuesta...?   por hora   por día
***kwan**to **kwes**ta...*   *por **o**-ra*   *por **dee**-a*

What do you do in your spare time? *(familiar)*
¿Qué haces en tu tiempo libre?
*ke **a**-thes en too **tyem**po **lee**-bre*

I like...   **painting**   **sunbathing**
Me gusta...   pintar   tomar el sol
*me **goo**sta...*   *pin**tar***   *to**mar** el sol*

I like...   **sport**
Me gustan...*(plus plural)*   los deportes
*me **goo**stan...*   *los de**por**-tes*

Do you like playing...? *(polite)*   **Do you like...?** *(familiar)*
Le gusta jugar a...?   Te gusta...?
*le **goo**sta khoo**gar** a...*   *te **goo**sta...*

■ CINEMA ■ MUSIC ■ SPORTS ■ TELEVISION ■ WALKING

17 May 1994	17 de mayo de 1994
Dear Sirs	Muy señores míos: *(commercial letter)*
Dear Sir / Madam	Muy señor mío / Muy señora mía:
Yours faithfully	Le(s) saluda atentamente
Dear Mr... / Dear Mrs...	Estimado Sr....: / Estimada Sra....:
Yours sincerely	Saludos cordiales
Dear Rosa	Querida Rosa:
Best regards	Un abrazo
Dear Pepe	Querido Pepe:
Love	Un fuerte abrazo *or* Besos

Further to your letter of 7 May...
Con relación a su carta del 7 de mayo...

Further to our telephone conversation...
Con relación a nuestra conversación telefónica...

Please find enclosed...
Le adjunto... / Le adjuntamos... *(writing on behalf of a company)*

Thank you for the information / your price list
Le agradezco su información / su lista de precios

We are very sorry, but we are unable to...
Lamentamos no poder...

I look forward to hearing from you
A la espera de sus noticias

by return [of] post
a vuelta de correo

■ **FAX** ■ **OFFICE**

BAGGAGE RECLAIM	LA RECOGIDA DE EQUIPAJE
LEFT LUGGAGE OFFICE	LA CONSIGNA
LUGGAGE TROLLEY	EL CARRITO

My luggage hasn't arrived
No ha llegado mi equipaje
*no a lye**ga**-do mee ekee-**pa**-khe*

My suitcase has arrived damaged
Me ha llegado la maleta estropeada
*me a lye**ga**-do la ma-**le**ta estrope-a-da*

What's happened to the luggage on the flight from…?
¿Qué ha pasado con el equipaje del vuelo de…?
*ke a pa**sa**-do kon el ekee-**pa**-khe del **bwe**lo de…*

Can you help me with my luggage, please?
¿Me puede ayudar con el equipaje, por favor?
*me **pwe**-de ayoo-**dar** kon el ekee-**pa**-khe por fa**bor***

When does the left luggage office open / close?
¿Cuándo abren / cierran la consigna?
*kwan*do **a**-bren / **thye**-rran la kon-**seeg**na*

I'd like to leave this suitcase…
Quisiera dejar esta maleta…
*kee-**sye**-ra de**khar** es*ta ma-**le**ta…*

until … o'clock
hasta las…
*as*ta las…*

overnight
por la noche
*por la **no**-che*

till Saturday
hasta el sábado
*as*ta el **sa**-bado*

Can I leave my luggage here?
¿Puedo dejar aquí el equipaje?
***pwe**do de**khar** a-**kee** el ekee-**pa**-khe*

I'll collect it at…
Vengo a recogerlo a las…
***ben**go a reko-**kher**lo a las…*

■ **YOU MAY HEAR**

Puede dejarlo aquí hasta las seis
pwe-de de**khar**-lo a-**kee** **a**sta las **se**-ees*
You may leave it here until 6 o'clock

■ **AIR TRAVEL**

54

*In this section we have used the familiar form **tu** for the questions.*

What's your name?	**My name is...**
¿Cómo te llamas?	Me llamo...
komo te lya-mas	*me lya-mo...*
How old are you?	**I'm ... years old**
¿Cuantos años tienes?	Tengo ... años
kwantos a-nyos tye-nes	*tengo ... a-nyos*
Are you Spanish?	**I'm English / Scottish / Welsh**
¿Eres español(a)?	Soy inglés(a) / escocés(a) / galés(a)
e-res espa-nyol(a)	*soy een-gles(a) / esko-thes(a) / ga-les(a)*
Where do you live?	**Where do you live?** *(plural)*
¿Dónde vives?	¿Dónde vivís?
don-de bee-bes	*don-de bee-bees*
I live in London	**We live in Glasgow**
Vivo en Londres	Vivimos en Glasgow
beebo en lon-dres	*beebee-mos en glasgow*
I'm still studying	**I work** **I'm retired**
Todavía estoy estudiando	Trabajo Estoy jubilado(a)
toda-bee-a estoy estoo-dyan-do	*tra-bakho estoy khoobee-lado(a)*

I'm...	**single**	**married**	**divorced**
Estoy...	soltero(a)	casado(a)	divoricado(a)
estoy...	*sol-tero(a)*	*ka-sado(a)*	*dee-bor-thyado(a)*

I have...	**a boyfriend**	**a girlfriend** **a partner**
Tengo...	novio	novia pareja
tengo...	*nobyo*	*nobya pa-rekha*
I have ... children		**I have no children**
Tengo ... hijos		No tengo hijos
tengo ... eekhos		*no tengo eekhos*
I'm here...	**on holiday**	**for work**
Estoy aquí...	de vacaciones	por razones de trabajo
estoy a-kee...	*de baka-thyo-nes*	*por ratho-nes de traba-kho*

■ LEISURE/INTERESTS ■ SPORTS ■ WEATHER ■ WORK

Have you...?   **a map of** *(name town)*   **a map of the region**
¿Tiene...?   un plano de...   un mapa de esta zona
tye-ne ...   *oon plano de...*   *oon mapa de esta thona*

Can you show me where ... is on the map?
¿Puede indicarme dónde está ... en el mapa?
pwe-de eendee-kar-me don-de esta ... en el mapa

Do you have a detailed map of the area?
¿Tiene algún mapa detallado de la zona?
tye-ne al-goon mapa deta-lyado de la thona

Can you draw me a map?
¿Me puede hacer un plano?
me pwe-de a-ther oon plano

Do you have a guide book / a leaflet in English?
¿Tiene alguna guía / algún folleto en inglés?
tye-ne al-goona gee-a / al-goon folye-to en een-gles

I'd like the English language version *(of a cassette guide)*
Quisiera la versión inglesa (del casete)
kee-sye-ra la ver-syon een-gle-sa (del ka-sete)

Where can I/we buy an English newspaper?
¿Dónde se puede comprar periódicos ingleses?
don-de se pwe-de komprar peree-o-deekos een-gle-ses

Do you have any English newspapers / novels?
¿Tiene periódicos ingleses / novelas inglesas?
tye-ne peree-o-deekos een-gle-ses / nobe-las een-gle-sas

When do the English newspapers arrive?
¿Cuándo llegan los periódicos ingleses?
kwando lye-gan los peree-o-deekos een-gle-ses

Please reserve *(name newspaper)* **for me**
¿Me reserva el..., por favor?
me re-serba el... por fabor

■ DIRECTIONS ■ SIGHTSEEING & TOURIST OFFICE

■ LIQUIDS

1/2 litre... *(c.1 pint)*	medio litro de...	*me*dyo *lee*tro de...
a litre of...	un litro de...	oon *lee*tro de...
1/2 bottle of...	media botella de...	*me*dya bo-*te*lya de ...
a bottle of...	una botella de...	oona bo *te*lya de...
a glass of...	un vaso de...	oon *ba*so de...

■ WEIGHTS

100 grams	cien gramos de...	thyen *gra*mos de...
1/2 kilo of... *(c.1 lb)*	medio kilo de...	*me*dyo *kee*lo de...
a kilo of...	un kilo de...	oon *kee*lo de...

■ FOOD

a slice of...	una loncha de...	oona *lon*cha de...
a portion of...	una ración de...	oona ra-*thyon* de...
a dozen...	una docena de...	oona do-*the*na de...
a box of...	una caja de...	oona *ka*kha de...
a packet of...	un paquete de...	oon pa-*ke*-te de...
a tin of...	una lata de...	oona *la*ta de...
a jar of...	un tarro de...	oon *ta*rro de...

■ MISCELLANEOUS

1000 pts worth of...	mil pesetas de...	meel pe-*se*tas de...
a third	un tercio	oon *ter*thyo
a quarter	un cuarto	oon *kwar*to
ten per cent	el diez por ciento	el dyeth por *thyen*to
more...	más...	mas
less...	menos...	*me*nos
enough	bastante	bas*tan*-te
double	el doble	el *do*-ble
twice	dos veces	dos *be*-thes
three times	tres veces	tres *be*-thes

■ FOOD ■ SHOPPING

You can buy either **un billete de 10 viajes**, *which is valid for 10 journeys or* **un abono transporte**, *which covers a month's travel on both bus and metro.*

ENTRADA	ENTRANCE
SALIDA	WAY OUT / EXIT
LÍNEA DE METRO	METRO LINE

Where is the nearest metro station?
¿Dónde está la estación de metro más próxima?
don-de esta la esta-**thyon** de **me**tro mas **prok**-seema

How does the ticket machine work?
¿Cómo funciona la máquina de billetes?
komo foon-**thyo**na la **ma**-keena de bee-**lye**-tes

I'm going to...
Voy a...
boy a...

Do you have a map of the metro?
¿Tiene un plano del metro?
tye-ne oon **pla**no del **me**tro

How do I/we get to...?
¿Cómo se va a...?
komo se ba a...

Do I have to change?
¿Tengo que cambiar de línea?
tengo ke kam**byar** de **lee**-ne-a

Which line is it for...?
¿Qué línea es para ir a...?
ke **lee**-ne-a es para eer a...

In which direction?
¿En qué dirección?
en ke deerek-**thyon**

What is the next stop?
¿Cuál es la próxima parada?
kwal es la **prok**-seema pa-**ra**da

Excuse me!
¡Oiga, perdone!
oyga perdo-**ne**

Please let me through
¿Me deja pasar?
me **de**kha pa**sar**

I'm getting off here
Me bajo aquí
me **ba**kho a-**kee**

■ BUS ■ TAXI

Banks are generally open 0900-1400 Monday to Friday, with some banks open on Saturday mornings. Double-check opening hours when you arrive as these change during the summer.

CAJERO AUTOMÁTICO	CASH DISPENSER
INTRODUZCA LA TARJETA	INSERT YOUR CARD
TECLEE SU NÚMERO PERSONAL	ENTER YOUR PERSONAL NUMBER
SACAR DINERO	CASH WITHDRAWAL
OPERACIÓN EN PROCESO	WE ARE DEALING WITH YOUR REQUEST
ESPERE	PLEASE WAIT

Where can I/we change some money?
¿Dónde se puede cambiar dinero?
*don-de se **pwe**-de kam**byar** dee-**ne**ro*

I want to change these traveller's cheques
Quiero cambiar estos cheques de viaje
*kye-ro kam**byar** es-tos **che**-kes de **bya**-khe*

When does the bank open?
¿Cuándo abren el banco?
*kwan-do a-bren el **ban**ko*

When does the bank close?
¿Cuándo cierran el banco?
*kwan-do **thye**-rran el **ban**ko*

Can I pay with pounds / dollars?
¿Puedo pagar con libras / dólares?
*pwe-do pa**gar** kon **lee**bras / **do**la-res*

Can I use my credit card to get pesetas?
¿Puedo obtener pesetas con la tarjeta de crédito?
*pwe-do ob-te**ner** pe-**se**tas kon la tar-**khe**ta de **kre**-deeto*

Can I use my card with this cash dispenser?
¿Puedo usar mi tarjeta en este cajero automático?
*pwe-do oo**sar** mee tar-**khe**ta en **es**te ka-**khe**ro owto-**ma**tee-ko*

Do you have any loose change?
¿Tiene dinero suelto?
*no **tye**-ne dee-**ne**ro **swel**to*

■ PAYING

Are there any good concerts on?
¿Dan algún buen concierto aquí?
dan al-goon bwen kon-thyerto a-kee

Where can I get tickets?
¿Dónde venden las entradas?
don-de ben-den las en-tradas

Where can we hear some flamenco / salsa?
¿Qué sitios hay para escuchar flamenco / salsa?
ke seetyos a-ee para eskoo-char fla-menko / salsa

What sort of music do you like?
¿Qué música le gusta?
ke moo-seeka le goosta

I like...
Me gusta...
me goosta...

Which is your favourite group?
¿Qué grupo le gusta más?
ke groopo le goosta mas

Who is your favourite singer?
¿Qué cantante le gusta más?
ke kantan-te le goosta mas

Can you play any musical instruments?
¿Sabe tocar algún instrumento musical?
sabe tokar al-goon eenstroo-men-to moo-seekal

I play...	**the guitar**	**piano**	**clarinet**
Yo toco...	la guitarra	el piano	el clarinete
yo toko...	*la geeta-rra*	*el pya-no*	*el kla-reene-te*

Have you been to any good concerts recently?
¿Ha ido a algún concierto bueno últimamente?
ha eedo a al-goon kon-thyerto bweno ool-teema-mente

Do you like opera?
¿Le gusta la ópera?
le goosta la o-pera

Do you like reggae? *(familiar)*
¿Te gusta el reggae?
te goosta el reggae

■ ENTERTAINMENT ■ MAKING FRIENDS

0	cero	*the*ro
1	uno	*oo*no
2	dos	dos
3	tres	tres
4	cuatro	*kwa*tro
5	cinco	*theen*ko
6	seis	*se*-ees
7	siete	*sye*-te
8	ocho	*o*-cho
9	nueve	*nwe*-be
10	diez	dyeth
11	once	*on*-the
12	doce	*do*-the
13	trece	*tre*-the
14	catorce	ka*tor*-the
15	quince	*keen*-the
16	dieciséis	dyethee-*se*-ees
17	diecisiete	dyethee-*sye*-te
18	dieciocho	dyethee-*o*-cho
19	diecinueve	dyethee-*nwe*-be
20	veinte	*be*-een-te
21	veintiuno	be-eentee-*oo*-no
22	veintidós	be-eentee-*dos*
23	veintitrés	be-eentee-*tres*
24	veinticuatro	be-eentee-*kwa*tro
25	veinticinco	be-eentee-*theen*ko
26	veintiséis	be-eentee-*se*-ees
27	veintisiete	be-eentee-*sye*-te
28	veintiocho	be-eentee-*o*-cho
29	veintinueve	be-eentee-*nwe*be
30	treinta	*tre*-eenta
40	cuarenta	kwa-*ren*ta
50	cincuenta	theen-*kwen*ta
60	sesenta	se-*sen*ta
70	setenta	se-*ten*ta
80	ochenta	o-*chen*ta
90	noventa	no-*ben*ta
100	cien	thyen
110	ciento diez	*thyen*to dyeth
500	quinientos	keen*yen*-tos
1,000	mil	meel
2,000	dos mil	dos meel
1 million	un millón	oon mee-*lyon*

1st	primero	pree-*mero*
2nd	segundo	se-*goon*do
3rd	tercero	tér-*the*ro
4th	cuarto	*kwar*to
5th	quinto	*keen*to
6th	sexto	*seks*to
7th	séptimo	*sep*-teemo
8th	octavo	ok-*ta*bo
9th	noveno	no-*ben*o
10th	décimo	*de*-theemo

| AN APPOINTMENT | UNA CITA |
| SWITCHBOARD | LA CENTRALITA |

I'd like to speak to the office manager
Quisiera hablar con el jefe (la jefa) de oficina
kee-*sye*-ra a-*blar* kon el *khe*fe (la *khe*fa) de ofee-*thee*na

What is your address?
¿Cuál es su dirección?
kwal es soo deerek-*thyon*

Which floor?
¿Qué piso es?
ke *pee*so es

Can you photocopy this for me?
¿Me puede fotocopiar esto?
me *pwe*-de foto-ko*pyar* *es*to

Do you use a courier service?
¿Disponen de servicio de mensajero?
dees-*po*nen de ser-*bee*thyo de mensa-*khe*ro

Can you send this for me?
¿Puede enviar esto por mí?
pwe-de en-*byar* *es*to por mee

What time does the office open / close?
A qué hora abren / cierran la oficina?
a ke *o*-ra *a*-bren / *thye*-rran la ofee-*thee*na

How do I get to your office?
¿Cómo se va a su oficina?
*ko*mo se ba a soo ofee-*thee*na

■ **YOU MAY HEAR**

Siéntese, por favor
syen-te-se por fa*bor*
Please take a seat

Ahora enseguida viene...
a-*o*-ra en-se*gee*-da *bye*-ne...
...will be with you in just a moment

■ **BUSINESS–MEETING** ■ **FAX** ■ **LETTERS**

AMOUNT TO BE PAID	EL IMPORTE
BILL	LA CUENTA
CASH DESK	LA CAJA
INVOICE	LA FACTURA
PAY AT THE CASH DESK	ABONE EL IMPORTE EN CAJA
RECEIPT	EL RECIBO

How much is it?
¿Cuánto es?
kwanto es

How much will it be?
¿Cuánto me costará?
kwanto me kos-tara

Can I pay...?
¿Se puede pagar...?
se pwe-de pagar...

by credit card
con tarjeta de crédito
kon tar-kheta de kre-deeto

by cheque
con talón
kon talon

Do you take credit cards?
¿Aceptan tarjetas de crédito?
a-theptan tar-khetas de kre-deeto

Is service included?
¿Está incluido el servicio?
esta eenkloo-ee-do el ser-beethyo

Is VAT included?
¿Está incluido el IVA?
esta eenkloo-ee-do el ee-ba

Put it on my bill
Póngalo en mi cuenta
ponga-lo en mee kwenta

I need a receipt, please
Necesito un recibo, por favor
ne-the-seeto oon re-theebo por fabor

Do I pay in advance?
¿Se paga por adelantado?
se paga por a-delan-tado

Where do I pay?
¿Dónde se paga?
don-de se paga

I'm sorry
Lo siento
lo syento

I've nothing smaller
No tengo nada cambiado
no tengo nada kam-byado

■ MONEY ■ SHOPPING

SÚPER	4 STAR
SIN PLOMO	UNLEADED
GASOIL / GASÓLEO	DIESEL
GASOLINA	PETROL
SURTIDOR	PETROL PUMP

Is there a petrol station near here?
¿Hay una estación de servicio por aquí?
*a-ee oona esta-**thyon** de ser-**bee**thyo por a-**kee***

Fill it up, please
Lleno, por favor
lyeno por fabor

Can you check the oil / the water?
¿Me revisa el aceite / el agua?
*me re**bee**-sa el a-**the**-ee-te / el a**gwa***

...pesetas worth of unleaded petrol
...pesetas de gasolina sin plomo
*...pe-**se**tas de gaso-**lee**na seen **plo**mo*

Where is...?	**the air line**	**the water**
¿Dónde está...?	el aire	el agua
***don**-de esta...*	*el a-**ee**-re*	*el a**gwa***

Can you check the tyre pressure, please?
¿Me revisa la presión de los neumáticos, por favor?
*me re**bee**-sa la pre-**syon** de los ne-oo-**ma**tee-kos por fa**bor***

Please fill this can with petrol
Por favor, ¿me llena esta lata de gasolina?
*por fa**bor** me **lye**na **es**ta **la**ta de gaso-**lee**na*

Can I pay with this credit card?
¿Puedo pagar con esta tarjeta de crédito?
***pwe**do pa**gar** kon **es**ta tar-**khe**ta de **kre**-deeto*

■ **YOU MAY HEAR**

¿Qué surtidor ha usado?
*ke soor-tee-**dor** a oo**sa**-do*
Which pump did you use?

■ **BREAKDOWNS** ■ **CAR**

FARMACIA (green cross)	PHARMACY / CHEMIST
FARMACIA DE GUARDIA	DUTY CHEMIST
RECETA MÉDICA	PRESCRIPTION

I don't feel well
Me encuentro mal
me en-kwentro mal

Have you something for...?
¿Tiene algo para...?
tye-ne algo para...

a headache
el dolor de cabeza
el dolor de ka-betha

car sickness
el mareo de coche
el ma-re-o de ko-che

diarrhoea
la diarrea
la dee-a-rre-a

I have a rash
Me ha salido un sarpullido
me a sa-leedo oon sar-poolyee-do

Is it safe for children?
¿Lo pueden tomar los niños?
lo pwe-den tomar los neenyos

How much should I give?
¿Cuánto le doy?
kwanto le doy

■ YOU MAY HEAR

Tómelo tres veces al día antes / con / después de la comida
to-melo tres be-thes al dee-a an-tes / kon / des-pwes de la ko-meeda
Take it three times a day before / with / after meals

■ WORDS YOU MAY NEED

antiseptic	el antiséptico	*antee-septee-ko*
aspirin	la aspirina	*aspee-reena*
condoms	los preservativos	*pre-serba-teebos*
dental floss	la seda dental	*seda dental*
period pains	las molestias de la regla	*moles-tyas de la regla*
plasters	las tiritas®	*tee-reetas*
sanitary pads	las compresas	*kom-presas*
sore throat	el dolor de garganta	*dolor de gar-ganta*
tampons	los tampones	*tampo-nes*
toothpaste	la pasta de dientes	*pasta de dyen-tes*

■ BODY ■ DOCTOR

Tapes for video cameras and camcorders can be bought in photography shops, department stores and hypermarkets.

Where can I buy tapes for a video camera?
¿Dónde venden cintas para vídeo-cámaras?
don-de ben-den theentas para beede-o-kamaras

A colour film   **with 24 / 36 exposures**
Un carrete en color   de 24 / 36 fotos
oon ka-rre-te en kolor   de be-eentee-kwatro/tre-eenta-ee-se-ees fotos

A video tape for this video camera
Una cinta para esta vídeo-cámara
oona theenta para esta beede-o-kamara

Have you batteries…?   **for this camera / this video camera**
¿Tiene pilas…?   para esta cámara / esta vídeo-cámara
tye-ne peelas…   *para esta ka-mara / esta beede-o-kamara*

Can you develop this film?   **How much will it be?**
¿Me pueden revelar este carrete?   ¿Cuánto me va a costar?
me pwe-den re-belar este ka-rre-te   *kwanto me ba a kostar*

I'd like mat / glossy prints
Quería las copias en mate / en brillo
ke-ree-a las kopyas en mate / en bree-lyo

When will the photos be ready?
¿Para cuándo estarán las fotos?
para kwando esta-ran las fotos

The film is stuck   **Can you take it out for me?**
El carrete se ha trabado   ¿Puede sacármelo usted?
el ka-rre-te se a tra-bado   *pwe-de sakar-me-lo oosted*

Is it OK to take pictures here?
¿Se puede hacer fotos aquí?
se pwe-de a-ther fotos a-kee

Would you take a picture of us, please?
¿Podría usted hacernos una foto, por favor?
po-dree-a oosted a-thernos oona foto por fabor

■ SHOPPING

Main Post Offices are open in the mornings (0900-1300) and late afternoons (1700-1900) Mon.-Fri., and until 1400 on Saturdays.

POST OFFICE	LA OFICINA DE CORREOS
POSTBOX	EL BUZÓN
STAMPS	LOS SELLOS

Is there a post office near here?
¿Hay una oficina de Correos por aquí?
*a-ee oon ofee-thee*na de ko-**rre**-os por a-**kee**

Which counter sells stamps?
¿En qué ventanilla venden los sellos?
*en ke benta-nee*lya **ben**-den los **se**lyos

Can I have stamps for ... postcards to Great Britain
Me da sellos para ... postales para Gran Bretaña
*me da **se**lyos para ... posta-les para gran bre-**ta**nya*

I want to send this letter registered post
Quiero mandar esta carta certificada
***kye**ro man**dar es**ta **kar**ta thertee-fee**ka**-da*

How much is it to send this parcel?
¿Cuánto cuesta mandar este paquete?
***kwan**to **kwes**ta man**dar es**te pa-**ke**-te*

by air	**by surface mail**
por avión	por correo normal
*por a-**byon***	*por ko-**rre**-o nor**mal***

It's a gift	**The value of contents is ... pesetas**
Es un regalo	El valor es de ... pesetas
*es oon re-**ga**lo*	*el ba**lor** es de ... pe-**se**tas*

■ YOU MAY HEAR

Rellene este impreso
*re-**lye**ne **es**te eem-**pre**so*
Fill in this form

■ DIRECTIONS

Can you help me?
¿Me puede ayudar?
me pwe-de ayoo-dar

I only speak a little Spanish
Solo hablo un poco de español
solo a-blo oon poko de espa-nyol

Does anyone here speak English?
¿Hay aquí alguien que hable inglés?
a-ee a-kee algyen ke a-ble een-gles

What's the matter?
¿Qué pasa?
ke pasa

I would like to speak to whoever is in charge
Quiero hablar con el(la) encargado(a)
kyero a-blar kon el(la) en-karga-do(a)

I'm lost
Me he perdido
me e per-deedo

How do I get to...?
¿Cómo voy a...?
komo boy a...

I've missed...	**my train**	**my plane**	**my connection**
He perdido...	el tren	el avión	el enlace
c pcr deedo...	*el tren*	*el a-byon*	*el enla-the*

I've missed my flight because there was a strike
He perdido el vuelo porque había una huelga
e per-deedo el bwelo porke abee-a oona welga

The coach has left without me
Se ha ido el autocar y me ha dejado aquí
se a eedo el owto-kar ee me a de-khado a-kee

Can you show me how this works?
¿Me puede enseñar como funciona esto?
me pwe-de en-se-nyar komo foon-thyona esto

I have lost my purse
He perdido el monedero
e per-deedo el mone-dero

I need to get to...
Tengo que ir a...
tengo ke eer a...

Leave me alone!
¡Déjeme en paz!
de-khe-me en path

Go away!
¡Váyase!
baya-se

■ COMPLAINTS ■ EMERGENCIES

Do you have...?
¿Tiene(n)...?
tye-ne(n)...

When...?
¿Cuándo...?
kwando...

At what time...?
¿A qué hora...?
a ke o-ra...

Where is / are...?
¿Dónde está / están...?
don-de esta / es-tan...

Can I...?
¿Puedo...?
pwedo...

May we...?
¿Podríamos...?
po-dree-amos...

Is it...?
¿Es...? / ¿Está...?
es... / esta...

Are they...?
¿Son...? / ¿Están...?
son... / estan...

Is / Are there...?
¿Hay...?
a-ee...

Is it far?
¿Está lejos?
esta lekhos

What time is it?
¿Qué hora es?
ke o-ra es

Who are you?
¿Quién es usted?
kyen es oosted

Who...?
¿Quién...?
kyen...

What...?
¿Qué...?
ke...

Why...?
¿Por qué...?
por ke...

How many...?
¿Cuántos(as)...?
kwantos(as)...

How much is it?
¿Cuánto es?
kwanto es

How...?
¿Cómo...?
komo...

Which one?
¿Cuál?
kwal

Where are the toilets?
¿Dónde están los aseos?
don-de estan los a-seos

■ BASICS

| REPARACIÓN DE CALZADO | SHOE REPAIR SHOP |
| REPARACIONES EN EL ACTO | REPAIRS WHILE YOU WAIT |

This is broken
Se me ha roto esto
se me a roto esto

Where can I get this repaired?
¿Dónde me lo pueden arreglar?
don-de me lo pwe-den a-rre-glar

Is it worth repairing?
¿Merece la pena arreglarlo?
me-rethe la pena a-rre-glarlo

Can you repair...?
¿Puede usted arreglarme...?
pwe-de oosted a-rre-glarme...

these shoes
estos zapatos
estos tha-patos

my watch
el reloj
el relo

How much will it be?
¿Cuánto me costará?
kwanto me kos-tara

Can you do it straightaway?
¿Me lo puede hacer en el acto?
me lo pwe-de a-ther en el akto

How long will it take to repair?
¿Cuánto tardan en arreglarlo?
kwanto tardan en a-rre-glarlo

When will it be ready?
¿Para cuándo está?
para kwando esta

Where can I have my shoes reheeled?
¿Dónde me pueden poner tapas a los zapatos?
don-de me pwe-den poner tapas a los tha-patos

I need some...
Necesito un poco de...
ne-the-seeto oon poko de...

glue
pegamento
pega-mento

Sellotape®
celo
thelo

Do you have a needle and thread?
¿Tiene hilo y una aguja?
tye-ne eelo ee oona a-gookha

The lights have fused
Se ha ido la luz
se a eedo la looth

■ **BREAKDOWNS**

Come in!
¡Pase!
pa-se

Please come back later
Por favor, vuelva más tarde
por fabor bwel-ba mas tarde

I'd like breakfast in my room
Quisiera desayunar en la habitación
kee-sye-ra desa-yoonar en la abee-tathyon

Please bring...
Por favor,¿me trae...?
por fabor me tra-e...

a glass
un vaso
oon baso

clean towels
toallas limpias
to-a-lyas leem-pyas

toilet paper
papel higiénico
papel ee-khye-neeko

I'd like an early morning call tomorrow
Quisiera que me llamaran temprano, mañana por la mañana
kee-sye-ra ke me lya-ma-ran tem-prano ma-nyana por la ma-nyana

At 6 o'clock	At 6.30	At 7 o'clock
A las seis	A las seis y media	A las siete
a las se-ees	*a las se-ees ee medya*	*a las sye-te*

I'd like an outside line
Quisiera llamar fuera
kee-sye-ra lya-mar fwera

The ... doesn't work
El/La ... no funciona
el/la ... no foonthyo-na

Please can you repair it
Pueden arreglarlo/la?
pwe-den a-rre-glarlo/la

I need more coat hangers
Necesito más perchas
ne-the-seeto mas per-chas

Do you have a laundry service?
¿Tienen servicio de lavandería?
tye-nen ser-beethyo de laban-deree-a

LIQUIDACIÓN / REBAJAS	SALE / REDUCTIONS
HOY, ABIERTO HASTA LAS...	OPEN TODAY TILL...

How do I/we get to the main shopping area?
¿Cómo se va a la zona principal de tiendas?
*ko*mo se ba a la **tho**na preenthee-**pal** de **tyen**das

I'm looking for a present for...
Estoy buscando un regalo para...
estoy boos-**kan**do oon re-**ga**lo para...

my mother
mi madre
mee **ma**dre

a child
un niño
oon **nee**nyo

Where can I buy...?
¿Dónde puedo comprar...?
don-de **pwe**do kom**prar**...

toys
juguetes
khoo-**ge**-tes

gifts
regalos
re-**ga**los

Can you recommend any good shops?
¿Puede recomendarme alguna tienda buena?
pwe-de reko-men**dar**-me al-**goon**a **tyen**da **bwe**na

Which floor are shoes on?
¿En qué planta están los zapatos?
en ke **plan**ta es**tan** los tha-**pa**tos

I'd like something similar to this
Quería algo parecido a esto
ke-**ree**-a **al**go pa-re-**thee**do a **es**to

It's too expensive for me
Me resulta demasiado caro
me re-**sool**ta dema-**sya**do **ka**ro

Have you anything else?
¿No tiene otra cosa?
no **tye**-ne **o**-tra **ko**sa

Is there a market?
¿Hay mercado?
a-ee mer-**ka**do

Which day?
¿Qué día?
ke **dee**-a

■ YOU MAY HEAR

¿Qué desea?
ke de**se**-a
Can I help you?

¿Algo más?
algo mas
Would you like anything else?

■ CLOTHES ■ MEASUREMENTS & QUANTITIES

Most shops close for lunch approx. 1330-1630 and stay open till about 2030. Department stores remain open all day.

baker's	PANADERÍA	pana-de**ree**-a
bookshop	LIBRERÍA	lee-bre**ree**-a
butcher's	CARNICERÍA	karneo the-**ree**-a
cake shop	PASTELERÍA	pastele-**ree**-a
clothes *(women's)*	ROPA DE SEÑORA	**ro**pa de se-**nyo**ra
clothes *(men's)*	ROPA DE CABALLERO	**ro**pa de kabal-**lyer**o
clothes *(children's)*	ROPA DE NIÑOS	**ro**pa de **neen**yos
dry-cleaner's	TINTORERÍA / LIMPIEZA EN SECO	teento-re**ree**-a / leem-**pye**-tha en **se**ko
electrical goods	ELECTRICIDAD	elek-treethee-**dad**
fishmonger's	PESCADERÍA	peska-de**ree**-a
furniture	MUEBLES	**mwe**bles
gifts	REGALOS	re-**ga**los
greengrocer's	FRUTERÍA	froo-te**ree**-a
grocer's	TIENDA DE COMESTIBLES	**tyen**da de ooltra-komes-**tee**-bles
hairdresser's	PELUQUERÍA	peloo-ke**ree**-a
health food shop	ALIMENTOS NATURALES	alee-**men**tos natoo-**ra**les
household *(goods)*	HOGAR MENAJE	ho**gar** me-**na**khe
ironmonger's	FERRETERÍA	fe-rrete-**ree**-a
jeweller's	JOYERÍA	kho-ye**ree**-a
market	MERCADO	mer-**ka**do
pharmacy	FARMACIA	far-**ma**thya
self-service	AUTOSERVICIO	owto-ser**bee**-thyo
shoe shop	ZAPATERÍA	tha-pa-te**ree**-a
shop	TIENDA	**tyen**da
sports shop	DEPORTES	de-**por**tes
stationer's	PAPELERÍA	pa-pe-le**ree**-a
supermarket	SUPERMERCADO	soo-permer-**ka**do
sweet shop	CONFITERÍA	konfeeter-**ee**-a
tobacconist's	ESTANCO	es-**tan**ko
toy shop	JUGUETERÍA	kho-gete-**ree**-a

*The tourist office is called **la oficina de turismo**. If you are looking for somewhere to stay they should have details of hotels, campsites, etc.*

Where is the tourist office?
¿Dónde está la oficina de turismo?
*don-de esta la ofee-**thee**na de too-**ree**smo*

What can we visit in the area?
¿Qué podemos visitar en esta zona?
*ke po-**de**mos bee-seetar en esta thona*

Have you any leaflets?
¿Tiene algún folleto?
*tye-ne al-**goon** fo-**lye**to*

When can we visit the...?
¿Cuándo se puede ir a ver el/la...?
kwando se pwe-de eer a ber el/la...

We'd like to go to...
Nos gustaría ir a...
*nos goosta-**ree**-a eer a*

Are there any excursions?
¿Hay alguna excursión organizada?
*a-ee al-**goo**na exkoor-**syon** or-ganee-**tha**da*

When does it leave?
¿A qué hora sale?
*a ke **o**-ra **sa**-le*

Where does it leave from?
¿De dónde sale?
*de **don**-de **sa**-le*

How much does it cost to get in?
¿Cuánto cuesta entrar?
kwan**to **kwes**ta en-**trar

Are there any reductions for...?
¿Hacen descuento a...?
*a-then des-**kwen**to a...*

children	students	unemployed	senior citizens
los niños	los estudiantes	los parados	los jubilados
*los **nee**nyos*	*los estoo-**dyan**-tes*	*los pa-**ra**dos*	*los khoo-beel**a**dos*

■ ENTERTAINMENT ■ MAPS, GUIDES & NEWSPAPERS

English	Spanish	
ABIERTO OPEN	**DEGUSTACIÓN** TASTING	**PROHIBIDO BAÑARSE** NO BATHING
ABONE EL IMPORTE EN CAJA PAY AT THE CASH DESK	**EMPUJAR** PUSH	**PROHIBIDO FUMAR** NO SMOKING
AGUA POTABLE DRINKING WATER	**ENTRADA** ENTRANCE	**REBAJAS** SALES
ANDÉN PLATFORM	**FECHA** DATE	**LIQUIDACIÓN** SALE
ASCENSOR LIFT	**FRÍO** COLD	**SALIDA** EXIT
ASEOS TOILETS	**FUMADORES** SMOKING	**SE ALQUILA** FOR HIRE, TO RENT
AUTOSERVICIO SELF-SERVICE	**INFORMACIÓN** INFORMATION	**SEÑORAS** LADIES
CABALLEROS GENTS	**LIBRE** FREE, VACANT	**SERVICIOS** TOILETS
CAJA CASH DESK	**NO FUNCIONA** OUT OF ORDER	**SE VENDE** FOR SALE
CALIENTE HOT	**NO TOCAR** DO NOT TOUCH	**SÓTANO** BASEMENT
CERRADO CLOSED	**OCUPADO** ENGAGED	**TAQUILLA** TICKET OFFICE
COMPLETO NO VACANCIES	**PLANTA BAJA** GROUND FLOOR	**TIRAR** PULL
CONSIGNA LEFT LUGGAGE	**PLAZAS LIBRES** VACANCIES	**SE RUEGA NO FUMAR** NO SMOKING PLEASE
DAMAS LADIES	**PRIVADO** PRIVATE	**URGENCIAS** CASUALTY DEPT.
	PROHIBIDO EL PASO NO ENTRY	

SKI PASS	EL "FORFAIT"
INSTRUCTOR	EL MONITOR / LA MONITORA
CROSS-COUNTRY SKIING	EL ESQUÍ DE FONDO

I want to hire skis
Quería alquilar unos esquíes
ke**ree**-a alkee-**lar** **oo**nos es**kee**-es

Does the price include...?	**boots**	**poles**
¿El precio incluye...?	las botas	los bastones?
el **pre**thyo eenkloo-ye...	las **bo**tas	los bas-**to**nes

Can you adjust my bindings, please?
¿Me puede ajustar las fijaciones?
me **pwe**-de a-khoos-**tar** las feekha-**thyo**-nes

How much is a pass...?	**for a day**	**per week**
¿Cuánto cuesta un "forfait"...?	para un día	semanal
kwanto **kwes**ta oon for-**fa**-ee...	para oon **dee**-a	sema-**nal**

Do you have a map of the ski runs?
¿Tiene un mapa de pistas?
tye-ne oon **ma**pa de **pees**tas

When does the last chair-lift go up?
¿Cuándo sale el último telesilla?
kwando **sa**-le el **ool**-teemo tele-**see**-lya

■ **YOU MAY HEAR**

¿Ha esquiado alguna vez, antes?
a eskee-**a**-do al-**goo**na veth **an**-tes
Have you ever skied before?

¿De qué largura quiere los esquíes?
de ke lar-**goo**ra **kye**re los es**kee**-es
What length skis do you want?

¿Qué número de zapato usa?
ke **noo**-mero de tha-**pa**to **oo**sa
What is your shoe size?

MATCH / GAME	EL PARTIDO / EL JUEGO
PITCH / COURT	EL CAMPO / LA PISTA
TO DRAW A MATCH	EMPATAR

Where can I/we...?
¿Dónde se puede...?
*don-de se **pwe**-de...*

play tennis
jugar al tenis
*khoo**gar** al **te**nees*

play golf
jugar al golf
*khoo**gar** al golf*

go swimming
ir a nadar
*eer a na**dar***

go jogging
hacer "footing"
*a-**ther foo**teen*

see some pelota
ver jugar a pelota
*ber khoo**gar** a **pe**lo-ta*

How much is it per hour?
¿Cuánto cuesta por hora?
kwanto kwesta por o-ra

Do you have to be a member?
¿Hay que ser socio?
*a-ee ke ser **so**-thyo*

Do they hire out...?
¿Alquilan ...?
*al**kee**-lan...*

rackets
raquetas
*ra-**ke**tas*

golf clubs
palos de golf
palos de golf

We'd like to go to see *(name team)* **play**
Nos gustaría ir a ver jugar al...
*nos goosta-**ree**-a eer a ber khoo**gar** al...*

Where can we get tickets?
¿Dónde venden las entradas?
don-de ben-den las en-tradas

How do we get to the stadium?
¿Cómo se va al estadio?
komo se ba al es-tadyo

Which is your favourite football team? *(familiar)*
¿Qué equipo de fútbol te gusta más?
ke e-keepo de footbol te goosta mas

What sports do you play? *(familiar)*
¿Qué deportes practicas?
ke depor-tes prak-teekas

■ LEISURE/INTERESTS ■ SKIING ■ WALKING

All these items can be bought at **la papelería**

biro	el bolígrafo	*bolee-grafo*
book	el libro	*leebro*
card *(greetings)*	la tarjeta de felicitación	*tar-kheta de felee-thee-tathyon*
cardboard	la cartulina	*kartoo-leena*
crayons *(wax)*	las pinturas de cera	*peen-tooras de thera*
envelopes	los sobres	*so-bres*
exercise book	el cuaderno	*kwa-derno*
felt-tip pen	el rotulador	*rotoo-lador*
folder	la carpeta	*kar-peta*
glue	el pegamento	*pega-mento*
ink	la tinta	*teenta*
ink cartridge	el cartucho de tinta	*kar-toocho de teenta*
magazine	la revista	*re-beesta*
newspaper	el periódico	*peree-o-deeko*
note pad	el bloc de notas	*blok de notas*
paints	las pinturas	*peen-tooras*
paper	el papel	*papel*
paperback	el libro de bolsillo	*leebro de bol-seelyo*
paperclip	el clip	*kleep*
pen	la pluma / el bolígrafo	*plooma / bolee-grafo*
pencil	el lápiz	*lapeeth*
pencil sharpener	el sacapuntas	*saka-poontas*
rubber	la goma (de borrar)	*goma (de borrar)*
ruler	la regla	*regla*
Sellotape®	el celo	*thelo*
sheet of paper	la hoja de papel	*o-kha de papel*
stapler	la grapadora	*grapa-dora*
staples	las grapas	*grapas*
writing paper	el papel de escribir	*papel de eskree-beer*

■ OFFICE   ■ SHOPPING

PARADA DE TAXIS	TAXI RANK

I need a taxi
Necesito un taxi
ne-the-seeto oon taksee

Where can I/we get a taxi?
¿Dónde se cogen los taxis?
don-de se ko-khen los taksees

Please order me a taxi
Por favor, ¿me pide un taxi?
por fabor me peede oon taksee

straightaway
ahora enseguida
a-o-ra en-segee-da

for *(time)*
para las...
para las...

How much will it cost by taxi...?
¿Cuánto puede costar ir en taxi ...?
kwanto pwe-de kostar cer en taksee ...

to the centre
al centro
al thentro

to the station
a la estación
a la esta-thyon

to the airport
al aeropuerto
al a-ero-pwerto

to this address
a esta dirección
a esta deerek-thyon

Please take me/us to...
Me/Nos lleva a ..., por favor
me/nos lye-ba a ... por fabor

How much is it?
¿Cuánto es?
kwanto es

Why are you charging me so much?
¿Cómo me cobra tanto?
komo me ko-bra tanto

It's more than on the meter
Es más de lo que marca el contador
es mas de lo ke marka el kon-tador

Keep the change
Quédese con la vuelta
ke-de-se kon la bwelta

Sorry, I don't have any change
Lo siento, no tengo nada cambiado
lo syento no tengo nada kambya-do

I'm In a hurry
Tengo mucha prisa
tengo moocha pree-sa

Is it far?
¿Está lejos?
esta lekhos

I have to catch...
Tengo que coger...
tengo ke kho-kher...

the ... o'clock flight to...
el vuelo de las ... para...
el bwelo de las ... para...

■ BUS ■ METRO

*To phone Spain from the UK, the international code is **00 34** plus the Spanish area code (e.g. Barcelona-**3**, Madrid-**1**) followed by the number you require. To phone the UK from Spain, dial **07**, wait for the tone, then dial **44** plus the UK area code less the first 0, e.g., London (0)**171** or (0)**181**.*

PHONECARD	LA TARJETA TELEFÓNICA
TELEPHONE DIRECTORY	LA GUÍA TELEFÓNICA
YELLOW PAGES	LAS PÁGINAS AMARILLAS
ANSWERING MACHINE	EL CONTESTADOR AUTOMÁTICO
COLLECT CALL	LA LLAMADA A COBRO REVERTIDO
DIAL THE NUMBER	MARCAR EL NÚMERO
TO PICK UP / TO HANG UP	COGER / COLGAR

I want to make a phone call
Quiero hacer una llamada telefónica
*kyero a-**ther** oona lya-**ma**da te-le**fo**-neeka*

What coins do I need?
¿Qué monedas se necesitan?
*ke mo-**ne**das se ne-the-**see**tan*

Can you show me how this phone works?
¿Puede indicarme cómo funciona este teléfono?
*pwe-de eendee-**kar**-me **ko**mo foon-**thyo**na **es**te te-**le**-fono*

Where can I buy a phone card?
¿Dónde venden tarjetas telefónicas?
*don-de **ben**-den tar-**khe**tas te-le**fo**-neekas*

Señor Lopez, please
El Señor López, por favor
*el se**nyor lo**pez por fa**bor***

Extension...(number)
Extensión...
*es-ten**syon**...*

Can I speak to...?
¿Puedo hablar con...?
*pwe-do a-**blar** kon...*

I would like to speak to...
Quería hablar con...
*ke-**ree**-a a-**blar** kon...*

This is Jim Brown
Soy Jim Brown
soy jim brown

Speaking
Al habla
*al **a**-bla*

I want to make an outside call, can I have a line?
Quería llamar fuera, ¿Me da línea?
ke-**ree**-a lya**mar** **fwe**ra me da **lee**-ne-a

I'll call back...
Le volveré a llamar...
le **bol**be-**re** a lya**mar**...

later
más tarde
mas **tar**de

tomorrow
mañana
ma-**nya**na

We were cut off
Se ha cortado
se a kor-**ta**do

I can't get through
No consigo hablar
no kon-**see**go a-**blar**

■ YOU MAY HEAR

Diga
deega
Hello

¿Con quién hablo?
kon kyen **a**-blo
Who am I talking to?

¿De parte de quién?
de **par**-te de kyen
Who's calling?

Un momento
oon mo-**men**to
Just a moment

No cuelgue, por favor
no **kwel**ge por fa**bor**
Hold on, please

Ahora se pone
a-**o**-ra se **po**ne
He/She is coming

Está comunicando
esta komoo-nee**kan**-do
It's engaged

¿Puede volver a llamar más tarde?
pwe de bol**ber** a lya**mar** mas **tar**de
Can you try again later?

¿Quiere dejar algún recado?
kye-re de**khar** al-**goon** re-**ka**do
Do you want to leave a message?

Se ha equivocado de número
se a ekee-bo**ka**-do de **noo**-mero
You've got a wrong number

Este es el contestador automático de...
este es el kon-testa-**dor** owto-**ma**tee-ko de...
This is the answering machine of...

Deje su mensaje después de oir la señal
dekhe soo men**sa**-khe des-**pwes** de o-**eer** la se**nyal**
Please leave a message after the tone

■ BUSINESS–MEETING ■ FAX ■ OFFICE

REMOTE CONTROL	EL MANDO A DISTANCIA
SOAP	LA TELENOVELA
VIDEO RECORDER	EL VIDEO
NEWS	EL TELEDIARIO / LAS NOTICIAS
TO SWITCH ON	ENCENDER
TO SWITCH OFF	APAGAR
PROGRAMME	EL PROGRAMA
CARTOONS	LOS DIBUJOS ANIMADOS

Where is the television?
¿Dónde está el televisor?
don-de esta el te-lebee-sor

How do you switch it on?
¿Cómo se enciende?
ko-mo se enthyen-de

Which button do I press?
¿Qué botón tengo que pulsar?
ke boton ten-go ke pool-sar

Please could you lower the volume?
Por favor, ¿podría bajar el volumen?
por fabor pod-ree-a bakhar el boloo-men

May I turn the volume up?
¿Puedo subir el volumen?
pwedo soobeer el boloo-men

What's on television?
¿Qué ponen en la televisión?
ke po-nen en la te-lebee-syon

When is the news?
¿Cúando es el telediario?
kwando es el tele-dyaryo

Do you have any English-speaking channels?
¿Hay alguna cadena en inglés?
a-ee al-goo-na ka-de-na en een-gles

When are the children's programmes?
¿Cuándo hay programas infantiles?
kwando a-ee pro-gra-mas een-fantee-les

Do you have any English videos?
¿Tiene algún vídeo en inglés?
a-ee al-goon beede-o en een-gles

PLAY	LA OBRA DE TEATRO
STALLS	BUTACAS DE PATIO
CIRCLE	PRINCIPAL
UPPER CIRCLE	ANFITEATRO
SEAT	LA LOCALIDAD / EL SITIO
CLOAKROOM	EL GUARDARROPA

What's on at the theatre?
¿Qué obras de teatro ponen?
ke **o**-bras de te-a-tro **po**-nen

How do we get to (name)**...?**
¿Cómo se va al teatro...?
komo se ba al te-a-tro...

What prices are the tickets?
¿De qué precios son las entradas?
de ke pre**thyos** son las en-**tra**das

I'd like two tickets...
Quisiera dos entradas...
kee-**sye**-ra dos en-**tra**das...

for tonight
para esta noche
para **esta no**-che

for tomorrow night
para mañana por la noche
para ma-**nya**na por la **no**-che

for 5th August
para el cinco de agosto
para el **theen**ko de a-**gos**to

in the stalls
de butacas de patio
de boo-**ta**kas de **pa**tyo

in the circle
de principal
de preenthee-**pal**

in the upper circle
de anfiteatro
de anfe-te-**a**-tro

How long is the interval?
¿Cuánto dura el descanso?
kwanto **doo**ra el des-**kan**so

Is there a bar?
¿Hay bar?
a-ee bar

When does the performance begin / end?
¿Cúando empieza / termina la representación?
kwando em-**pye**tha / ter-**mee**na la re-presen-ta**thyon**

I enjoyed the play
Me ha gustado mucho la obra
me a goos-**ta**do **moo**cho la **o**-bra

It was very good
Ha sido muy buena
a **see**do mwee **bwe**na

■ ENTERTAINMENT ■ LEISURE/INTERESTS

*The 24-hour clock is used a lot more in Europe than in Britain. After 1200 midday, it continues: **1300–las trece**, **1400–las catorce**, **1500–las quince**, etc. until **2400–las veinticuatro**. With the 24-hour clock, the words **cuarto** (quarter) and **media** (half) aren't used:*

13.15 (1.15pm)	*las trece quince*	
19.30 (7.30pm)	*las diecinueve treinta*	
22.45 (10.45pm)	*las veintidós cuarenta y cinco*	

What time is it, please?	**am**	**pm**
¿Qué hora es, por favor?	de la mañana	de la tarde
*ke **o**-ra es por fa**bor***	*de la ma-**nya**na*	*de la **tar**-de*

It's ...	**2 o'clock**	**3 o'clock**	**6 o'clock** (etc.)
Son...	las dos	las tres	las seis
son...	*las dos*	*las tres*	*las **se**-ees*

It's 1 o'clock	**It's 1200 midday**	**At midnight**
Es la una	Son las doce del mediodía	A medianoche
*es la **oo**na*	*son las **do**-the del medyo-**dee**-a*	*a medya **no**-che*

9	**las nueve**
	*las **nwe**be*
9.10	**las nueve y diez**
	*las **nwe**be ee dyeth*
quarter past 9	**las nueve y cuarto**
	*las **nwe**be ee **kwar**to*
9.20	**las nueve y veinte**
	*las **nwe**be ee be-**een**-te*
9.30	**las nueve y media**
	*las **nwe**be ee **me**dya*
9.35	**las diez menos veinticinco**
	*las dyeth **me**nos be-eentee-**theen**ko*
quarter to 10	**las diez menos cuarto**
	*las dyeth **me**nos **kwar**to*
10 to 10	**las diez menos diez**
	*las dyeth **me**nos dyeth*

■ NUMBERS

When does it open / close?
¿Cuándo abren / cierran?
*kwan*do *a-*bren / *thye-*rran

When does it begin / finish?
¿Cuándo empieza / termina?
*kwan*do em-*pye*tha / ter-*mee*na

at 3 o'clock
a las tres
a las tres

before 3 o'clock
antes de las tres
*an-*tes de las tres

after 3 o'clock
después de las tres
des-*pwes* de las tres

today
hoy
oy

tonight
esta noche
*esta no-*che

tomorrow
mañana
ma-*nya*na

yesterday
ayer
a-*yer*

the day before yesterday
anteayer
ante-a-*yer*

the day after tomorrow
pasado mañana
pa-*sa*do ma-*nya*na

in the morning
por la mañana
*por la ma-nya*na

this morning
esta mañana
*esta ma-nya*na

in the afternoon
por la tarde *(until dusk)*
*por la tar-*de

in the evening
por la tarde / por la noche *(late evening or night)*
*por la tar-de / por la no-*che

at half past 7
a las siete y media
a las *sye-*te ee *med*ya

at about 10 o'clock
a eso de las diez
a *e*so de las dyeth

in an hour's time
dentro de una hora
*den*tro de oona *o*-ra

in a while
dentro de un rato
*den*tro de oon *ra*to

two hours ago
hace dos horas
*a-*the dos *o-*ras

soon
pronto
*pron*to

early
temprano
tem-*pra*no

late
tarde
*tar-*de

later
más tarde
mas *tar-*de

I'll do it...
Lo haré...
lo a-*re*...

as soon as possible
lo antes posible
lo *an-*tes po*see-*ble

...at the latest
...lo más tarde
...lo mas *tar-*de

There are three types of tickets on the high-speed AVE train –
Club**, **Preferente *and* ***Turista***. *Prices vary according to time:* ***Punta***
(peak), ***Valle*** *(off-peak), and* ***Llano*** *(standard).* ***Días azules*** *are
cheaper days to travel.*

RENFE *(Red Nacional de Ferrocarriles Españoles)*	**SPANISH NATIONAL RAILWAYS**
TALGO / INTERCITY	**FAST TRAIN / INTERCITY**
SUPLEMENTO TREN	**SUPPLEMENT PAYABLE**
VÍA	**PLATFORM** *(written on timetables)*
ANDÉN	**PLATFORM**

When is the next train to....?
¿Cuándo es el próximo tren para…?
kwando es el prok-seemo tren para…

Two return tickets to...
Dos billetes de ida y vuelta a…
dos bee-lye-tes de eeda ee bwelta a…

A single to...
Un billete de ida a…
oon bee lye te de eeda a…

Tourist class
De clase turista
de klase too-reesta

Smoking / Non smoking
Fumador / No fumador
fooma-dor / no fooma-dor

Is there a supplement to pay?
¿Hay que pagar suplemento?
a-ee ke pagar soo-ple-mento

I want to book a seat on the AVE to Seville
Quería reservar un asiento en el AVE a Sevilla
ke-ree-a re-serbar oon a-syento en el a-be a se-beelya

When is the first / last train to...?
¿Cuándo es el primer / el último tren para…?
kwando es el pree-mer / el ool-teemo tren para…

When does it arrive in...?
¿Cuándo llega a…?
kwando lyega a…

Do I have to change?
¿Tengo que hacer transbordo?
*ten*go ke a-*ther* trans-*bor*do

Where?
¿Dónde?
don-de

How long is there to get the connection?
¿Cuánto tiempo hay para el enlace?
*kwan*to *tyem*po *a*-ee para el enla-the

Which platform does it leave from?
¿De qué andén sale?
de ke an-*den* *sa*-le

Is this the right platform for the train to...?
¿Sale de este andén el tren para...?
sa-le de *es*te an-*den* el tren para...

Is this the train for...?
¿Es este el tren para...?
es *es*te el tren para...

When will it leave?
¿Cuándo va a salir?
*kwan*do ba a sa-*leer*

Why is the train delayed?
¿Por qué sale el tren con retraso?
por ke *sa*-le el tren kon re-*tra*so

Does the train stop at...?
¿Para el tren en...?
pa-ra el tren en...

Please let me know when we get to...
Por favor, ¿me avisa cuando lleguemos a...?
por fa*bor* me a*bee*-sa *kwan*do lye-*ge*mos a...

Is there a buffet on the train?
¿Hay servicio de cafetería en el tren?
a-ee ser-*beet*hyo de ka-fe-te*ree*-a en el tren

Is this free? *(seat)*
¿Está libre?
es*ta* *lee*bre

Excuse me
¡Perdón!
per-*don*

LUGGAGE

Don't expect great things – the Spanish love good meat!

Are there any vegetarian restaurants here?
¿Hay aquí algún restaurante vegetariano?
a-ee a-__kee__ al-__goon__ restow-__ran__-te be-kheta-__rya__no

Do you have any vegetarian dishes?
¿Tienen algún plato vegetariano?
__tye__-nen al-__goon pla__to be-kheta-__rya__no

Which dishes have no meat / fish?
¿Cuáles son los platos que no llevan carne / pescado?
__kwa__-les son los __pla__tos que no __lye__ban __kar__-ne / pes-__ka__do

What fish dishes do you have?
¿Qué tienen de pescado?
ke __tye__-nen de pes-__ka__do

I'd like pasta as a main course
De segundo, quisiera tomar pasta
de se-__goon__do kee-__sye__ra to__mar pas__ta

I don't like meat	**What do you recommend?**
No me gusta la carne	¿Qué me recomienda?
no me __goo__sta la __kar__-ne	*ke me reko-__myen__da*

Is it made with vegetable stock?
¿Está hecho con caldo de verduras?
es__ta e__-cho kon __kal__do de ber-__doo__ras

■ **POSSIBLE DISHES**

berenjenas *aubergines*
ensalada *salad*
espárragos *asparagus*
gazpacho *cold cucumber, peppers, garlic and tomato soup*
pisto *peppers, courgettes, onions cooked in a tomato sauce*
judias verdes *French beans*
revuelto de champiñones *mushrooms with scrambled eggs*
revuelto de espinacas *spinach with scrambled eggs*
tortilla española *omelette with potato and onions*

■ **EATING OUT**

Are there any guided walks?
¿Organizan recorridos a pie con guía?
*orga-**nee**than reko-**rree**dos a pye kon **gee**-a*

Do you have details?
¿Me puede dar información?
*me **pwe**-de dar eentor-ma**thyon***

Do you have a guide to local walks?
¿Tiene alguna guía de esta zona que traiga recorridos a pie?
***tye**-ne al-**goo**na **gee**-a de esta **tho**na ke tra-**ee**-ga reko-**rree**dos a pye*

How many kilometres is the walk?
¿De cuántos kilómetros es la excursión?
*de **kwan**tos kee**lo**-metros es la exkoor-**syon***

How long will it take?
¿Cuántas horas se puede tardar?
kwan**tas **o**-ras se **pwe**-de tar**dar

Is it very steep?
¿Hay mucha subida?
*a-ee **moo**cha soo-**bee**da*

We'd like to go climbing
Nos gustaría hacer montañismo
*nos goosta-**ree**-a a-**ther** monta-**nyees**-mo*

Do we need walking boots?
¿Necesitamos botas de montaña?
*ne-the-**see**tamos **bo**tas de mon-**tan**ya*

Should we take...?
¿Hace falta llevar...?
*a-the **fal**ta lye**bar**...*

water
agua
*a**gwa***

food
comida
*ko-**mee**da*

waterproofs
impermeables
*eemper-me-**a**-bles*

a compass
una brújula
*oona **broo**-khoola*

What time does it get dark?
¿A qué hora anochece?
*a ke **o**-ra ano-**che**the*

■ MAPS, GUIDES... ■ SIGHTSEEING & TOURIST OFFICE

CHUBASCOS	SHOWERS
DESPEJADO	CLEAR
LLUVIA	RAIN
NIEBLA	FOG
NUBLADO	CLOUDY

It's sunny
Hace sol
a-the sol

It's raining
Está lloviendo
esta lyo-byendo

It's snowing
Está nevando
esta ne-bando

It's windy
Hace viento
a-the byento

What a lovely day!
¡Qué día más bueno!
ke dee-a mas bweno

What awful weather!
¡Qué tiempo tan malo!
ke tyempo tan malo

What will the weather be like tomorrow?
¿Qué tiempo hará mañana?
ke tyempo a-ra ma-nyana

Do you think it's going to rain?
¿Cree que va a llover?
kre-e ke ba a lyo-ber

Do I need an umbrella?
¿Necesitaré paraguas?
ne-the-seeta-re pa-ragwas

When will it stop raining?
¿Cuándo parará de llover?
kwando pa-rara de lyo-ber

It's very hot
Hace mucho calor
a-the moocho kalor

Do you think there will be a storm?
¿Cree que va a haber tormenta?
kre-e ke ba a a-ber tor-menta

Do you think it will snow?
¿Le parece que va a nevar?
le pa-rethe ke ba a nebar

What is the temperature?
¿Qué temperatura hace?
ke tem-pera-toora a-the

■ **MAKING FRIENDS**

90

The wine list, please
La carta de vinos, por favor
la **kar**ta de **bee**nos por fa**bor**

Can you recommend a good wine?
¿Puede recomendarnos un vino bueno?
pwe-de reko-men**dar**-nos oon **bee**no **bwe**no

A bottle...	**A carafe...**	**of the house wine**
Una botella...	Una jarra...	de vino de la casa
oona bo-**te**lya...	oona **kha**rra...	de **bee**no de la **ka**sa

of red wine	**of white wine**	**of rosé wine**
de vino tinto	de vino blanco	de vino rosado
de **bee**no **teen**to	de **bee**no **blan**ko	de **bee**no ro-**sa**do

of dry wine	**of sweet wine**	**of a local wine**
de vino seco	de vino dulce	de vino de la tierra
de **bee**no **se**ko	de **bee**no **dool**-the	de **bee**no de la **tye**rra

Albariño smooth white wine from Galicia

Alella dry, medium-dry white wines from Cataluña

Alicante strong country reds and **Fondillón**, aged mature wine

Cariñena mainly red wines, best drunk young, from Aragón

Cava good quality sparkling white wine from Penedés

Cigales light, fruity, dry rosé wines from Castilla-León

Jumilla strong, dark red wines from Murcia

Lágrima one of the best of the **Málaga** wines, very sweet

La Mancha firm whites and reds from Castilla-La Mancha

Málaga fortified, sweet, dark dessert wine

Navarra full-bodied reds from Navarra

Penedés fine reds, rosés and whites. Home of **Cava**

Ribeiro young, fresh, white wines from Galicia

Ribera del Duero fruity rosés and deep distinguished reds from
the banks of the river Duero in Castilla-León

Rioja some of the finest red wines of Spain: full-bodied, rich and
aged in oak. Also good white Riojas aged in oak

Valdepeñas soft, fruity, red wines and white wines

CONT

■ TYPES OF SHERRY   JEREZ

Fino *light, dry sherry, usually served chilled as an apéritif*
Amontillado *dry, nutty, amber sherry made from matured* **fino**
Oloroso *a dark, rich sherry which has been aged. It is often sweetened and sold as a cream sherry*
Palo cortado *midway between an* **oloroso** *and a* **fino**

■ OTHER DRINKS

What liqueurs do you have?
  ¿Qué licores tienen?
  *ke lee**ko**-res **tye**-nen*

Anís *aniseed-flavoured liqueur*
Coñac *Spanish brandy*
Orujo *strong spirit made from grape pressings*
Pacharán *sloe brandy*
Ron *rum*
Sangría *red wine, brandy, lemonade and fruit served chilled*
Sidra *dry cider from Asturias*

■ DRINKING ■ EATING OUT

What work do you do?
¿En qué trabaja?
*en ke tra**ba**-kha*

Do you enjoy it?
¿Le gusta?
*le **goo**sta*

I'm...	a doctor	a teacher	a secretary
Soy...	médico(a)	profesor(a)	secretaria
soy...	*me **deeko**(a)*	*pro-te**sor**(a)*	*se-kre**ta**-rya*

I work in...	a shop	a factory	a bank
Trabajo en...	una tienda	una fábrica	un banco
*tra**ba**-kho en...*	*oona **tyen**da*	*oona **fa**-breeka*	*oon **ban**ko*

I work from home
Trabajo en casa
*tra**ba**-kho en **ka**sa*

I'm self-employed
Trabajo por cuenta propia
*tra**ba**-kho por **cwen**ta **pro**-pee-a*

I have been unemployed for...
He estado en el paro...
*e es-**ta**do en el **pa**ro...*

...months
...meses
*...**me**ses*

It's very difficult to get a job at the moment
Ahora es muy difícil encontrar trabajo
*a-**o**-ra es mwee dee-**fee**theel en-kon**trar** tra**ba**-kho*

What are your hours?
¿Cuáles son sus horas de trabajo?
*kwa**les** son soos **o**-ras de tra**ba**-kho*

I work from 9 to 5
Trabajo de nueve a cinco
*tra**ba**-kho de **nwe**-be a **theen**ko*

from Monday to Friday
de lunes a viernes
*de **loo**-nes a **byer**-nes*

How much holiday do you get?
¿Cuánto tiempo tiene de vacaciones?
*kwan**to** **tyem**po **tye**-ne de baka-**thyo**-nes*

What do you want to be when you grow up?
¿Qué quieres hacer cuando seas mayor?
*ke **kye**-res a-**ther** kwan**do** **se**-as ma-**yor**

■ MAKING FRIENDS

NOUNS

Unlike English, Spanish nouns have a gender: they are either
masculine (**el**) or *feminine* (**la**). Therefore words for **the** and
a(n) must agree with the noun they accompany – whether
masculine, *feminine* or *plural*:

	masc.	fem.	plural
the	el gato	la plaza	los gatos, las plazas
a, an	un gato	una plaza	unos gatos, unas plazas

The ending of the noun will usually indicate whether it is
masculine or *feminine*:

-o or **-or** are generally *masculine*

-a, **-dad**, **-ión**, **-tud**, **-umbre** are generally *feminine*

NOTE: *feminine* nouns beginning with a stressed **a**- or **ha**- take
the *masculine* article **el**, though the noun is still *feminine*.

PLURALS

The articles **el** and **la** become **los** and **las** . Nouns ending with a
vowel become plural by adding **s** :

> el gato → los gatos
> la plaza → las plazas
> la calle → las calles

Where the noun ends in a consonant, then **-es** is added:

> el color → los colores
> la ciudad → las ciudades

Nouns ending in **-z** change their ending to **-ces** in the plural.

> el lápiz → los lápices
> la voz → las voces

ADJECTIVES

Adjectives normally follow the noun they describe in Spanish,
e.g. **la manzana roja (the red apple)**

Some common exceptions which go before the noun are:
buen good; **gran** great; **ningún** no, not any; **mucho** much,
many; **poco** little, few; **primer** first; **tanto** so much, so many,
e.g. **el último tren (the last train)**

Spanish adjectives also reflect the gender of the noun they describe. To make an adjective *feminine*, the *masculine* -**o** ending is changed to -**a** ; and the endings -**án**, -**ón**, -**or**, -**és** change to -**ana**, -**ona**, -**ora**, -**esa**:

masc. **el libro rojo**
(**the red book**)

fem. **la manzana roja**
(**the red apple**)

masc. **el hombre hablador**
(**the talkative man**)

fem. **la mujer habladora**
(**the talkative woman**)

To make an adjective plural an -**s** is added to the singular form if it ends in a vowel. If the adjective ends in a consonant, -**es** is added:

masc. **los libros rojos**
(**the red books**)

fem **las manzanas rojas**
(**the red apples**)

masc. **los hombres habladores**
(**the talkative men**)

fem **las mujeres habladoras**
(**the talkative women**)

MY, YOUR, HIS, HER

These words also depend on the gender and number of the noun they accompany and not on the sex of the 'owner'.

	with masc. sing. noun	*with fem. sing. noun*	*with plural nouns*
my	mi	mi	mis
your *(familiar sing.)*	tu	tu	tus
your *(polite sing.)*	su	su	sus
his/her/its	su	su	sus
our	nuestro	nuestra	nuestros/nuestras
your *(familiar pl.)*	vuestro	vuestra	vuestros/vuestras
their	su	su	sus
your *(polite pl.)*	su	su	sus

There is no distinction between **his** and **her** in Spanish:

su billete can mean either **his** or **her ticket**.

PRONOUNS

subject		*object*	
I	yo	**me**	me
you *(familiar sing.)*	tú	**you**	te
you *(polite sing.)*	usted (Vd.)	**you**	le
he/it	él	**him/it**	le, lo
she/it	ella	**her/it**	le, la
we	nosotros	**us**	nos
you *(familiar pl.)*	vosotros	**you**	os
you *(polite pl.)*	ustedes (Vds.)	**you**	les
they *(masc.)*	ellos	**them**	les, los
they *(fem.)*	ellas	**them**	les, las

Subject pronouns (**I**, **you**, **he**, etc.) are generally omitted in Spanish, since the verb ending distinguishes the subject:

hab**lo**	**I** speak
hab**lamos**	**we** speak

However, they are used for emphasis or to avoid confusion:

yo voy a Mallorca y **él** va a Alicante
I am going to Mallorca and **he** is going to Alicante

Object pronouns are placed before the verb in Spanish:

la veo	I see **her**
los conocemos	we know **them**

However, in commands or requests they follow the verb:

¡ayúda**me**!	help **me**!
escúcha**le**	listen **to him**

except when they are expressed in the negative:

¡no **me** ayudes!	don't help **me**
no **le** escuches	don't listen **to him**

The object pronouns shown above can be used to mean **to me**, **to us**, etc., but **to him/to her** is **le** and **to them** is **les**. If **le** and **les** occur in combinations with **lo/la/las/los** then **le/les** change to **se**, e.g. **se lo doy** (**I give it to him**)

VERBS

There are three main patterns of endings for Spanish verbs –
those ending **-ar**, **-er** and **-ir** in the dictionary.

	CANTAR	TO SING
	canto	I sing
	cantas	you sing
(usted)	canta	(s)he sings/you sing
	cantamos	we sing
	cantáis	you sing
(ustedes)	cantan	they sing/you sing

	VIVIR	TO LIVE
	vivo	I live
	vives	you live
(usted)	vive	(s)he lives/you live
	vivimos	we live
	vivís	you live
(ustedes)	viven	they live/you live

	COMER	TO EAT
	como	I eat
	comes	you eat
(usted)	come	(s)he eats/you eat
	comemos	we eat
	coméis	you eat
(ustedes)	comen	they eat/you eat

Like French, in Spanish there are two ways of addressing people:
the polite form (for people you don't know well or who are
older) and the familiar form (for friends, family and children). The
polite **you** is **usted** in the singular, and **ustedes** in the plural.
You can see from above that **usted** uses the same verb ending
as for **he** and **she**; **ustedes** the same ending as for **they**. Often
the words **usted** and **ustedes** are omitted, but the verb ending
itself indicates that you are using the polite form. The informal
words for **you** are **tú** (singular) and **vosotros** (plural).

THE VERB "TO BE"

There are two different Spanish verbs for **to be** – **ser** and **estar**.

Ser is used to describe a permanent state:

soy inglés	**I am English**
es una playa	**it is a beach**

Estar is used to describe a temporary state or where something is located:

how are you?	**¿cómo está?**
where is the beach?	**¿dónde está la playa?**

	SER	ESTAR	TO BE
	soy	estoy	**I am**
	eres	estás	**you are**
(usted)	es	está	**(s)he is/you are**
	somos	estamos	**we are**
	sois	estáis	**you are**
(ustedes)	son	están	**they are/you are**

Other common irregular verbs include:

	TENER	TO HAVE	IR	TO GO
	tengo	**I have**	voy	**I go**
	tienes	**you have**	vas	**you go**
(usted)	tiene	**(s)he has**	va	**(s)he goes**
	tenemos	**we have**	vamos	**we go**
	tenéis	**you have**	vais	**you go**
(ustedes)	tienen	**they have**	van	**they go**

	PODER	TO BE ABLE	QUERER	TO WANT
	puedo	**I can**	quiero	**I want**
	puedes	**you can**	quieres	**you want**
(usted)	puede	**(s)he can**	quiere	**(s)he wants**
	podemos	**we can**	queremos	**we want**
	podéis	**you can**	queréis	**you want**
(ustedes)	pueden	**they can**	quieren	**they want**

	HACER	TO DO	VENIR	TO COME
	hago	I do	vengo	I come
	haces	you do	vienes	you come
(usted)	hace	(s)he does	viene	(s)he comes
	hacemos	we do	venimos	we come
	hacéis	you do	venís	you come
(ustedes)	hacen	they do	vienen	they come

PAST TENSE

To form the simple past tense, **I gave/I have given**, **I finished/I have finished**, combine the present tense of the verb **haber – to have** with the past participle of the verb (**cantado, comido, vivido**):

	HABER	TO HAVE
	he	I have
	has	you have
(usted)	ha	(s)he has/you have
	hemos	we have
	habéis	you have
(ustedes)	han	they have/you have

e.g.	he cantado	I sang/I have sung
	ha comido	he ate/he has eaten
	hemos vivido	we lived/we have lived

To form a negative **no** is placed before all of the verb:

e.g.	no he cantado	I haven't sung
	no ha comido	he hasn't eaten
	no hemos vivido	we haven't lived

a	un(a)
abbey	la abadía
about (relating to)	acerca de
(approximately)	más o menos
above	arriba ; por encima
the flat above	*el piso de arriba*
accident	el accidente
accommodation	el alojamiento
ache	el dolor
my head aches	*me duele la cabeza*
adaptor (electrical)	el adaptador
address	la dirección
adhesive tape	la cinta adhesiva
admission charge	el precio de entrada
adult	el/la adulto(a)
advance: *in advance*	*por adelantado*
advertisement	el anuncio
advice	el consejo
after	después
afternoon	la tarde
aftershave	el aftershave
again	otra vez
against	contra
age	la edad
agency	la agencia
agent	el/la agente
ago: *a week ago*	*hace una semana*
air-conditioning	el aire acondicionado
airline	la línea aérea
air mail	el correo aéreo
air-mattress	el colchón de aire
airport	el aeropuerto
aisle	el pasillo
alarm	la alarma

alarm clock	el despertador
alcohol	el alcohol
alcoholic	alcohólico(a)
all	todo(a)/todos(as)
allergic to	alérgico(a) a
allow	permitir
all right *(agreed)*	de acuerdo
are you all right?	¿está bien?
almond	la almendra
almost	casi
alone	solo(a)
also	también
always	siempre
am	see **(to be)** GRAMMAR
ambulance	la ambulancia
America	América del Norte
American	norteamericano(a)
anaesthetic	la anestesia
and	y
angry	enfadado(a)
another	otro(a)
answer *n*	la respuesta
answer *vb*	responder
antibiotic	el antibiótico
antifreeze	el anticongelante
antiseptic	el antiséptico
any	alguno(a)
have you any pears?	¿tiene peras?
apartment	el apartamento
apéritif	el aperitivo
appendicitis	la apendicitis
apple	la manzana
appointment	la cita
approximately	aproximadamente

apricot	el albaricoque
are	*see* **(to be)** GRAMMAR
arm	el brazo
armbands *(swimming)*	los manguitos de nadar
armchair	el sillón
arrange	organizar
arrest *vb*	detener
arrival	la llegada
arrive	llegar
art gallery	la galería de arte
arthritis	el artritis
artichoke	la alcachofa
ashtray	el cenicero
ask *(for something)*	preguntar
(a favour)	pedir
asparagus	los espárragos
aspirin	la aspirina
asthma	el asma
at	a ; en
at home	en casa
attractive *(person)*	guapo(a)
aubergine	la berenjena
auction	la subasta
aunt	la tía
Australia	Australia
Australian	australiano(a)
author	el/la autor(a)
automatic	automático(a)
autumn	el otoño
avalanche	la avalancha
avocado	el aguacate
avoid *(obstacle)*	evitar
(person)	esquivar
awful	espantoso(a)

baby	el bebé
baby food	la comida para niños pequeños
babysitter	el/la canguro
bachelor	el soltero
back *(of body)*	la espalda
bacon	el beicon
bad *(weather, news)*	mal/malo(a)
(fruit and vegetables)	podrido(a)
bag	la bolsa
(suitcase)	la maleta
(handbag)	el bolso
baggage	el equipaje
baggage reclaim	la recogida de equipajes
bail bond	la garantía de fianza
baker's	la panadería
balcony	el balcón
bald	calvo(a)
ball	la pelota ; el balón
banana	el plátano
band *(rock)*	el grupo
bandage	la venda
bank	el banco
bar	el bar
barber's	la barbería
bark *vb (dog)*	ladrar
basket	la cesta
bath	el baño
to have a bath	*bañarse*
bathing cap	el gorro de baño
bathroom	el cuarto de baño
battery	la pila
(in car)	la batería
be	*see* **(to be)** GRAMMAR
beach	la playa

bean	la judía
(kidney bean)	la alubia
beautiful	hermoso(a)
bed	la cama
bedding	la ropa de cama
bedroom	el dormitorio
beef	la carne de vaca
beer	la cerveza
beetroot	la remolacha
before *(in time)*	antes de
(in place)	delante de
beggar	el/la mendigo(a)
begin	empezar
behind	detrás
behind the house	*detrás de la casa*
believe	creer
bell	la campana
(electric)	el timbre
below	debajo
belt	el cinturón
beside	al lado de
best	el/la mejor
better	mejor
between	entre
bicycle	la bicicleta
by bicycle	*en bicicleta*
big	grande
bigger	más grande
bikini	el bikini
bill	la cuenta
bin	el cubo
binoculars	los prismáticos
bird	el pájaro
birth	el nacimiento

birthday	el cumpleaños
birthday card	la tarjeta de cumpleaños
biscuit	la galleta
bit: *a bit of*	*un poco de*
bite	morder
(insect)	picar
bitter	amargo(a)
black	negro(a)
blackcurrant	la grosella negra
blade *(of razor)*	la cuchilla
blanket	la manta
bleach	la lejía
blind *adj*	ciego(a)
blister	la ampolla
blocked *(road)*	cortado(a)
(pipe)	obstruido(a)
blood	la sangre
blood group	el grupo sanguíneo
blouse	la blusa
blow-dry	el secado a mano
blue	azul
(light blue)	azul claro ; celeste
boarding card	la tarjeta de embarque
boarding house	la pensión
boat	el barco
boat trip	la excursión en barco
boil	hervir
boiled egg	*el huevo cocido*
bone	el hueso
book *n*	el libro
book *vb*	reservar
booking	la reserva
booking office	el despacho de billetes
bookshop	la librería

boot	la bota
(of car)	el maletero
border	la frontera
boring	aburrido(a)
boss	el jefe/la jefa
both	ambos(as)
bottle	la botella
bottle opener	el abrebotellas
box	la caja
box office	la taquilla
boy	el chico
boyfriend	el novio
bra	el sujetador
bracelet	la pulsera
brake	el freno
brake fluid	el líquido de frenos
brand	la marca
brandy	el coñac
bread	el pan
break vb	romper
breakable	frágil
breakdown	la avería
breakdown van	la grúa
breakfast	el desayuno
breast (chicken)	la pechuga
breathe	respirar
briefcase	la cartera
bridge	el puente
bring	traer
Britain	Gran Bretaña
British	británico(a)
brochure	el folleto
broken	roto(a)

broken down *(car, etc.)*	averiado(a)
brooch	el broche
broom	la escoba
brother	el hermano
brown	marrón
brush	el cepillo
Brussels sprouts	las coles de Bruselas
bucket	el cubo
buffet	la cafetería
buffet car	el coche-comedor
building	el edificio
bulb *(electric)*	la bombilla
bull	el torro
bullfight	la corrida de torros
bullfighter	el torero ; el matador
bullring	la plaza de torros
bun	el bollo
bureau de change	la oficina de cambio
burst *vb*	reventar
bus	el autobús *[Mexico* el camión*]*
business	los negocios
bus station	la estación de autobuses
bus stop	la parada de autobús
bus tour	la excursión en autobús/autocar
busy	ocupado(a)
but	pero
butcher's	la carnicería
butter	la mantequilla
button	el botón
buy	comprar
by *(via)*	por
(beside)	al lado de
bypass	la carretera de circunvalación

cabaret	el cabaret
cabbage	la col
cablecar	el teleférico
café	el café
cake	el pastel
calculator	la calculadora
call n (telephone)	la llamada
a long distance call	una llamada interurbana
call vb	llamar
(on telephone)	llamar por teléfono
calm	tranquilo(a)
camcorder	el vídeo-cámara
camera	la máquina de fotos ; la cámara
camp	acampar
campsite	el camping
can n	el bote
can vb (be able)	poder see GRAMMAR
can I …?	¿puedo …?
Canada	el Canadá
Canadian	canadiense
cancel	anular ; cancelar
canoe	la canoa
canoeing	el piragüismo
can opener	el abrelatas
car	el coche [Lat. Am. el carro]
carafe	la garrafa
caravan	la caravana
carburettor	el carburador
card (greetings)	la tarjeta
(playing)	el naipe ; la carta
cardigan	la chaqueta de punto
careful	cuidadoso(a)
be careful!	¡ten cuidado!
car ferry	el transbordador

car park	el aparcamiento
	[Lat. Am. **el estacionamiento**]
carpet	la alfombra
(fitted)	la moqueta
carriage (railway)	el vagón
carrot	la zanahoria
carry	llevar
car wash	el lavado (automático) de coches
case (suitcase)	la maleta
cash n	el dinero en efectivo
cash vb (cheque)	cobrar
cash desk	la caja
cashier	el/la cajero(a)
casino	el casino
cassette	el casete
castanets	las castañuelas
castle	el castillo
cat	el gato
catch (bus, train, etc.)	coger [Lat. Am. **tomar**]
cathedral	la catedral
Catholic	católico(a)
cauliflower	la coliflor
cause vb	provocar
cave	la cueva
celery	el apio
cemetery	el cementerio
centimetre	el centímetro
centre	el centro
century	el siglo
cereal (for breakfast)	los cereales
certain (sure)	seguro(a)
certificate	el certificado
chain	la cadena

chair	la silla
chairlift	el telesilla
chalet	el chalé ; el chalet
champagne	el champán
chance	la ocasión
change n	el cambio
(small coins)	suelto
(money returned)	la vuelta
change vb	cambiar
changing room	el probador
chapel	la capilla
charge n	el coste
charge vb	cobrar
cheap	barato(a)
cheaper	más barato(a)
check	revisar ; comprobar
check in (at airport)	facturar el equipaje
(at hotel)	registrarse
check-in desk	el mostrador de facturación
cheerio!	¡hasta luego!
cheers!	¡salud!
cheese	el queso
chemist's	la farmacia
cheque	el talón ; el cheque
cheque book	el talonario
cheque card	la tarjeta de identidad bancaria
cherry	la cereza
chestnut	la castaña
chewing gum	el chicle
chicken	el pollo
chickenpox	la varicela
child (boy)	el niño
(girl)	la niña

children *(infants)*	los niños
chilli	el chile ; la guindilla
chips	las patatas fritas
chocolate	el chocolate
chocolates	los bombones
chop *(meat)*	la chuleta
Christmas	la Navidad
Merry Christmas!	¡Felices Pascuas!
Christmas Eve	la Nochebuena
church	la iglesia
cider	la sidra
cigar	el puro
cigarette	el cigarrillo
cinema	el cine
circus	el circo
city	la ciudad
clean *adj*	limpio(a)
clean *vb*	limpiar
cleansing cream	la crema limpiadora
client	el/la cliente
climbing	el alpinismo
cloakroom	el guardarropa
clock	el reloj
close *adj (near)*	cercano(a)
close *vb*	cerrar
is it close?	¿está cerca?
closed	cerrado(a)
cloth *(rag)*	el trapo
clothes	la ropa
clothes peg	la pinza
cloudy	nublado(a)
clove	el clavo
club	el club

coach *(bus)*	el autocar
(train)	el coche ; el vagón
coach trip	la excursión en autocar
coast	la costa
coastguard	el guardacostas
coat	el abrigo
coat hanger	la percha
cocktail	el cóctel
cocoa	el cacao
coconut	el coco
coffee	el café
white coffee	*el café con leche*
black coffee	*el café solo*
coin	la moneda
Coke®	la Coca Cola®
colander	el escurridor de verduras
cold *n*	el resfriado
cold *adj*	frío(a)
I'm cold	*tengo frío*
colour	el color
comb	el peine
come	venir
(arrive)	llegar
come back	volver
come in	entrar
come in!	*¡pase! [Lat. Am. ¡siga!]*
comfortable	cómodo(a)
communion	la comunión
company	la compañía
compartment	el compartimento
complain	reclamar
complaint	la reclamación ; la queja
compulsory	obligatorio(a)
computer	el computador ; el ordenador

concert	el concierto
conditioner	el suavizante
condom	el preservativo
conductor *(on bus)*	el cobrador
conference	la conferencia
confirm	confirmar
congratulations	¡enhorabuena!
connect	conectar
connection *(train, etc.)*	el enlace
constipated	estreñido(a)
consulate	el consulado
contact	ponerse en contacto
contact lens cleaner	la solución limpiadora para lentes de contacto
contact lenses	las lentillas ; las lentes de contacto
contraceptive	el anticonceptivo
cook	cocinar
cooker	la cocina
cool	fresco(a)
copy *n*	la copia
copy *vb*	copiar
corkscrew	el sacacorchos
corner	la esquina
cortisone	la cortisona
cosmetics	los cosméticos
cost	costar
cot	la cuna
cotton	el algodón
cotton wool	el algodón hidrófilo
couchette	la litera
cough	la tos
country *(not town)*	el campo
(nation)	el país

couple *(2 people)*	la pareja
courgettes	los calabacines
courier *(tour guide)*	el/la guía de turismo
course *(of meal)*	el plato
cousin	el/la primo(a)
cover charge	el precio del cubierto
cow	la vaca
crab	el cangrejo
crash *(two cars, etc.)*	colisionar ; chocar
crash helmet	el casco protector
cream *(lotion)*	la crema
(on milk)	la nata
credit card	la tarjeta de crédito
crisps	las patatas fritas
cross *(road)*	cruzar
crossed line	el cruce de línea
crossroads	el cruce
crowded	concurrido(a)
cruise	el crucero
cucumber	el pepino
cup	la taza
cupboard	el armario
currant	la pasa
current	la corriente
cushion	el cojín
custard	las natillas
customer	el cliente/la clienta
customs	la aduana
cut *n*	el corte
cut *vb*	cortar
cutlery	los cubiertos
cycle *vb*	ir en bicicleta
cycling	el ciclismo

daily *(each day)*	cada día ; diario
damage	los daños
damp	húmedo(a)
dance *n*	el baile
dance *vb*	bailar
dangerous	peligroso(a)
dark	oscuro(a)
date	la fecha
date of birth	la fecha de nacimiento
daughter	la hija
day	el día
dead	muerto(a)
dear	querido(a)
(expensive)	caro(a)
decaffeinated coffee	el café descafeinado
deck chair	la tumbona
declare	declarar
deep	profundo(a)
deep freeze	el congelador
defrost	descongelar
de-ice	deshelar
delay	el retraso
delicious	delicioso(a)
dentist	el/la dentista
dentures	la dentadura postiza
deodorant	el desodorante
department stores	los grandes almacenes
departure	la salida
departure lounge	la sala de embarque
deposit	el depósito
dessert	el postre
details	los detalles
detergent	el detergente

detour	la desviación
develop	desarrollar
diabetic	diabético(a)
dialling code	el prefijo
diamond	el diamante
diarrhoea	la diarrea
diary	la agenda
dictionary	el diccionario
diesel	el gasoil ; el gasóleo
diet	el régimen
different	distinto(a)
difficult	difícil
dinghy	el velero ; el barco de vela
(rubber)	el bote neumático
dining room	el comedor
dinner	la cena
(have dinner)	cenar
direct (train, etc.)	directo(a)
directory	la guía telefónica
dirty	sucio(a)
disabled	minusválido(a)
disco	la discoteca
dish	el plato
dishtowel	el trapo
dishwasher	el lavaplatos
disinfectant	el desinfectante
distilled water	el agua destilada
divorced	divorciado(a)
dizzy	mareado(a)
do	hacer see GRAMMAR
doctor	el médico/la médica
documents	los documentos
dog	el perro
doll	la muñeca

dollar	el dólar
door	la puerta
double	doble
double bed	la cama de matrimonio
double room	la habitación doble
doughnut	el buñuelo
down	abajo
drains *(sewage system)*	el alcantarillado
draught	la corriente
dress *n*	el vestido
dress *vb (get dressed)*	vestirse
dressing *(for food)*	el aliño
drink *n*	la bebida
drink *vb*	beber
drinking chocolate	el chocolate caliente
drinking water	el agua potable
drive	conducir *[Lat. Am.* manejar*]*
driver *(of car)*	el/la conductor(a)
driving licence	el carné de conducir
drown	ahogarse
drug	la droga
drunk	borracho(a)
dry *adj*	seco(a)
dry *vb*	secar
dry-cleaner's	la tintorería ; la limpieza en seco
duck	el pato
due to	debido a
dummy	el chupete
during	durante
dust	el polvo
duty-free shop	la tienda libre de impuestos
duvet	el edredón
dynamo	la dinamo

each	cada
ear	la oreja ; el oído
earache	el dolor de oídos
I have earache	*me duele el oído*
earlier	antes
early	temprano
earn	ganar
earrings	los pendientes
earth	la tierra
earthquake	el terremoto
east	el este
Easter	la Pascua ; la Semana Santa
easy	fácil
eat	comer
edition	la edición
eel	la anguila
egg	el huevo
fried egg	*el huevo frito*
hard-boiled egg	*el huevo cocido*
scrambled eggs	*los huevos revueltos*
either: *either one*	*cualquiera de los dos*
elastic	el elástico
electric	eléctrico(a)
electrician	el/la electricista
electricity	la electricidad
electricity meter	el contador de la luz
embassy	la embajada
emergency	la emergencia
empty	vacío(a)
enclose	adjuntar
end	el fin
engaged *(to be married)*	prometido(a)
(toilet)	ocupado(a)
engine	el motor

engineer	el/la ingeniero(a)
England	Inglaterra
English	inglés/inglesa
enjoy: *enjoy your meal!*	¡que aproveche!
I enjoy swimming	me gusta nadar
enough	bastante
enquiry desk	la información
enter	entrar en
entertainments	los espectáculos
enthusiastic	entusiasta
entrance fee	el precio de entrada
envelope	el sobre
equipment	el equipo
escalator	la escalera mecánica
especially	especialmente
essential	imprescindible
Eurocheque	el Eurocheque
Europe	Europa
evening	la tarde
in the evening	por la tarde ; por la noche
evening meal	la cena
every	cada
everyone	todo el mundo
everything	todo
exact	exacto(a)
examination	el examen
example: *for example*	por ejemplo
excellent	excelente
except	excepto ; salvo
excess luggage	el exceso de equipaje
exchange *n*	el cambio
exchange *vb*	cambiar
exchange rate	el tipo de cambio
exciting	emocionado(a)

English	Spanish
exciting	emocionante
excursion	la excursión
excuse vb	perdonar
excuse me!	¡perdón!
exercise book	el cuaderno
exhibition	la exposición
exit	la salida
expect	esperar
expert	el/la experto(a)
expire (ticket, passport)	caducar
explain	explicar
express n (train)	el rápido
express: to send a	enviar una carta por correo
letter express	urgente
extra (in addition)	de más
(more)	adicional
eye	el ojo
eyelash	la pestaña

English	Spanish
fabric	la tela ; el tejido
face	la cara
facilities	los servicios
(equipment)	las instalaciones
factory	la fábrica
faint	desmayarse
fainted	desmayado(a)
fair (funfair)	el parque de atracciones
(hair)	rubio(a)
fake	falso(a)
fall	caer ; caerse
he/she has fallen	se ha caído
family	la familia
famous	famoso(a)

fan (electric)	el ventilador eléctrico
(paper)	el abanico
(football)	el/la hincha
(cinema, jazz, etc.)	el/la aficionado(a)
fan belt	la correa del ventilador
far	lejos
fare	el precio del billete
farm	la granja
farmer	el/la granjero(a)
farmhouse	la granja
fashionable	de moda
fast	rápido(a)
fat	gordo(a)
father	el padre
father-in-law	el suegro
fault (defect)	el defecto
favourite	favorito(a) ; preferido(a)
feather	la pluma
feed	dar de comer
feel	sentir
I don't feel well	no me siento bien
to feel sick	estar mareado
felt-tip pen	el rotulador
feminine	femenino(a)
fence	la cerca
ferry	el transbordador
fetch (bring)	traer
(go and get)	ir a buscar
fever	la fiebre
few	pocos(as)
a few	algunos(as)
fiancé(e)	el/la novio(a)
field	el campo
fight vb	luchar

file *(computer)*	el fichero
(nail)	la lima
fill	llenar
(fill in form)	rellenar
fill it up, please!	*lleno, por favor*
fillet	el filete
filling *(in tooth)*	el empaste
film *(at cinema)*	la película
(for camera)	el carrete
filter	el filtro
fine *(to be paid)*	la multa
finger	el dedo
finish	acabar
fire	el fuego ; el incendio
fire!	*¡fuego!*
fire brigade	los bomberos
fire extinguisher	el extintor
fireworks	los fuegos artificiales
first	primero(a)
first aid	los primeros auxilios
first class	de primera clase
first floor	el primer piso
first name	el nombre de pila
fish *n*	el pescado
fish *vb*	pescar
fishing rod	la caña de pescar
fit *adj (healthy)*	en forma
fit *vb (clothes)*	quedar bien
fix *(mend)*	arreglar
fizzy	gaseoso(a)
flask *(thermos)*	el termo
flat *(apartment)*	el apartamento
(level)	llano(a)
(battery)	descargado(a)

flat tyre	la rueda pinchada
flavour	el sabor
flea	la pulga
flight	el vuelo
flippers	las aletas
flood	la inundación
floor *(of building)*	el piso
(of room)	el suelo
flour	la harina
flower	la flor
flu	la gripe
fly	la mosca
fly sheet	el doble techo
fog	la niebla
foggy: *it's foggy*	*hay niebla*
foil	el papel de aluminio
fold *vb*	doblar
follow	seguir
food	comida ; alimentación
food poisoning	la intoxicación por alimentos
foot	el pie
on foot	*a pie*
football	el fútbol
for *(in exchange for)*	por
for you	*para usted*
foreign	extranjero(a)
forest	el bosque
forget	olvidar
forgive	perdonar
fork	el tenedor
(in road)	la bifurcación
form *(document)*	el impreso
fortnight	quince días
fountain	la fuente

fracture	la fractura
France	Francia
free (not occupied)	libre
(costing nothing)	gratis
freezer	el congelador
French	francés/francesa
French beans	las judías verdes
frequent	frecuente
fresh	fresco(a)
fridge	el frigorífico
fried	frito(a)
friend	el/la amigo(a)
frightenend	asustado(a)
fringe	el flequillo
from	de ; desde
front	la parte delantera
in front	delante
frozen (food)	congelado(a)
fruit	la fruta
fruit juice	el zumo
fruit salad	la ensalada de frutas ;
	[Lat Am. la macedonia
frying pan	la sartén
fuel	el carburante
fuel pump	el surtidor de gasolina
full	lleno(a)
full board	pensión completa
funeral	el entierro
funfair	el parque de atracciones
funny (amusing)	divertido(a)
(strange)	raro(a) ; curioso(a)
fur	el abrigo de pieles
furniture	los muebles
fuse	el fusible

gallery	la galería
gallon	= *approx. 4.5 litres*
gambling	el juego
game	el juego
garage	el garaje
garden	el jardín
garlic	el ajo
gas	el gas
gas cylinder	la bombona de gas
gears	las marchas
gentleman	el señor
gents *(toilets)*	los servicios de caballeros
genuine	auténtico(a)
German	alemán/alemana
German measles	la rubéola
Germany	Alemania
get *(obtain)*	obtener
(receive)	recibir
(fetch)	traer
get in *(vehicle)*	entrar (en) ; subir (al)
get off *(bus, metro, etc.)*	bajarse (del)
gift	el regalo
gift shop	la tienda de regalos
gin	la ginebra
ginger	el jengibre
girl	la chica
girlfriend	la novia
give	dar
give back	devolver
glass *(for drinking)*	el vaso
(substance)	el vidrio ; el cristal
glasses	las gafas *[Lat. Am.* los lentes*]*
gloves	los guantes
glucose	la glucosa

glue	el pegamento
go	ir
go back	volver
go down(stairs)	bajar
go in	entrar (en)
go out	salir
goggles	las gafas de bucear
(for skiing)	las gafas de esquí
gold	el oro
golf	el golf
golf course	el campo de golf
good	bueno(a)
good afternoon	¡buenas tardes!
goodbye	¡adiós!
good evening	¡buenas tardes/noches!
good morning	¡buenos días!
good night	¡buenas noches!
goose	el ganso
gramme	el gramo
grandfather	el abuelo
grandmother	la abuela
grape	la uva
grapefruit	el pomelo
grass	la hierba
greasy	grasiento(a)
green	verde
green card	la carta verde
grey	gris
grilled	a la parrilla
grocer's	la tienda de comestibles
ground	el suelo
ground floor	la planta baja
groundsheet	la tela impermeable

group	el grupo
guarantee	la garantía
guard *(on train)*	el jefe de tren
guest *(house guest)*	el/la invitado(a)
(in hotel)	el/la huésped(a)
guesthouse	la pensión
guide n	el/la guía
guide vb	guiar
guidebook	la guía turística
guided tour	la visita con guía
gym shoes	las playeras

haemorrhoids	las hemorroides
hair	el pelo
hairbrush	el cepillo para el pelo
haircut	el corte de pelo
hairdresser	el peluquero/la peluquera
hairdryer	el secador de pelo
hairgrip	la horquilla
hair spray	la laca
half	medio(a)
a half bottle of ...	*media botella de ...*
half board	media pensión
ham	el jamón
hand	la mano
handbag	el bolso
handicapped	minusválido(a)
handkerchief	el pañuelo
hand luggage	el equipaje de mano
hand-made	hecho(a) a mano
hangover	la resaca
happen	pasar
what happened?	*¿qué ha pasado?*

happy	feliz
harbour	el puerto
hard	duro(a)
hat	el sombrero
have	tener *see* GRAMMAR
hay fever	la fiebre del heno
hazelnut	la avellana
he	él *see* GRAMMAR
head	la cabeza
headache	el dolor de cabeza
head walter	el maître
hear	oír
heart	el corazón
heart attack	el infarto ; el ataque cardíaco
heater	el calentador
heating	la calefacción
heavy	pesado(a)
hello	¡hola!
(on telephone)	¡diga!
help *n*	la ayuda
help!	¡socorro!
help *vb*	ayudar
can you help me?	¿puede ayudarme?
herb	la hierba
here	aquí
high	alto(a)
high blood pressure	la tensión alta
high chair	la silla alta
high tide	la marea alta
hill	la colina
hill-walking	el montañismo
hire	alquilar
hit	pegar
hitchhike	hacer auto-stop

hold	sostener ; tener
(contain)	contener
hold-up *(traffic jam)*	el atasco
hole	el agujero
holiday	las vacaciones
(public)	la fiesta
on holiday	de vacaciones
home	la casa
honey	la miel
honeymoon	la luna de miel
hope	esperar
I hope so/not	espero que sí/no
hors d'oeuvre	los entremeses
horse	el caballo
hose	la manguera
hospital	el hospital
hot	caliente
I'm hot	tengo calor
it's hot (weather)	hace mucho calor
hotel	el hotel
hour	la hora
house	la casa
house wine	el vino de la casa
hovercraft	el aerodeslizador ; el "hovercraft"
how *(in what way)*	cómo
how much?	¿cuánto?
how many?	¿cuántos?
how are you?	¿cómo está?
hungry: *I'm hungry*	tengo hambre
hurry: *I'm in a hurry*	tengo prisa
hurt: *my back hurts*	me duele la espalda
husband	el marido
hydrofoil	el hidrofoil

I	yo *see* **GRAMMAR**
ice	el hielo
ice cream	el helado
iced *(drink)*	con hielo
iced coffee	*el café con hielo*
ice lolly	el polo
ice rink	la pista de patinaje
if	si
ignition	el encendido
ignition key	la llave de contacto
ill	enfermo(a)
immediately	inmediatamente ; en seguida
important	importante
impossible	imposible
in	en
in 10 minutes	*dentro de 10 minutos*
inch	la pulgada = *approx. 2.5 cm*
included	incluido(a)
indigestion	la indigestión
indoors	dentro
(at home)	en casa
infectious	contagioso(a)
information	la información
information office	la oficina de información turística
injection	la inyección
injury	la herida ; la lesión
injured	herido(a) ; lesionado(a)
ink	la tinta
insect	el insecto
insect bite	la picadura
insect repellent	la loción contra insectos
inside	el interior
inside the car	*dentro del coche*

instant coffee	el café instantáneo
instead of	en lugar de
instructor	el/la instructor(a) ; el/la monitor(a)
insulin	la insulina
insurance	el seguro
insurance certificate	el certificado de seguros
insure	asegurar
interesting	interesante
international	internacional
interpreter	el/la intérprete
interval *(theatre, etc.)*	el descanso ; el intermedio
interview	la entrevista
into	en
introduce	presentar
invitation	la invitación
invite	invitar
invoice	la factura
Ireland	Irlanda
Irish	irlandés/irlandesa
iron *n (for clothes)*	la plancha
(metal)	el hierro
iron *vb*	planchar
ironmonger's	la ferretería
is	ser/estar *see* GRAMMAR
island	la isla
it	lo/la *see* GRAMMAR
Italian	italiano(a)
Italy	Italia
itch	el picor
item	el artículo
itemized bill	la factura detallada
ivory	el marfil

jack (for car)	el gato
jacket	la chaqueta
jam (food)	la mermelada ; la confitura
jammed	atascado(a)
Japan	Japón
Japanese	japonés/japonesa
jar (container)	el tarro
jaundice	la ictericia
jazz	el jazz
jealous	celoso(a)
jeans	los vaqueros
jelly (dessert)	la gelatina
jellyfish	la medusa
jersey	el jersey
jeweller's	la joyería
jewellery	las joyas
Jewish	judío(a)
job	el empleo
jog (go jogging)	hacer "footing"
joint	la articulación
joke	la broma
journalist	el/la periodista
journey	el viaje
judge	el juez/la jueza
jug	la jarra
juice	el zumo
jump	saltar
jump leads	los cables para cargar la batería
junction (road)	la bifurcación
June	junio
just: just two	solamente dos
I've just arrived	acabo de llegar

keep	guardar ; mantener
keep the change	quédese con la vuelta
kennel	la caseta
kettle	el hervidor (de agua)
key	la llave
keyboard	el teclado
key in	teclear
key-ring	el llavero
kick	el puntapié
kid (young goat)	el cabrito
kidneys	los riñones
kill	matar
kilo	el kilo
kilometre	el kilómetro
kind n (sort, type)	la clase
kind adj (person)	amable
king	el rey
kiosk	el quiosco
kiss n	el beso
kiss vb	besar
kitchen	la cocina
kitten	el gatito
knee	la rodilla
knickers	las bragas
knife	el cuchillo
knit	hacer punto
knock vb (on door)	llamar
knock down (car)	atropellar
knot	el nudo
know (facts)	saber
(be acquainted with)	conocer
knowledge	los conocimientos

label	la etiqueta
laces (of shoe)	los cordones
ladder	la escalera de mano
ladies (toilet)	los servicios de señoras
lady	la señora
lager	la cerveza
lake	el lago
lamb	el cordero
lamp	la lámpara
land (piece of)	el terreno
lane	el camino
(of motorway)	el carril
language	el idioma
large	grande
last	último(a)
last week	*la semana pasada*
late	tarde
the train is late	*el tren viene con retraso*
sorry I'm late	*siento llegar tarde*
later	más tarde
launderette	la lavandería automática
laundry service	el servicio de lavandería
lavatory (in house)	el wáter
(in public place)	los aseos ; los servicios
lawyer	el/la abogado(a)
laxative	el laxante
layby	el área de aparcamiento
lazy	perezoso(a)
lead (electric)	el cable
leader	el/la líder
(guide)	el/la guía
leaf	la hoja
leak (of gas, liquid)	la fuga
(in roof)	la gotera

learn	aprender
least: *at least*	*por lo menos*
leather	la piel ; el cuero
leave *(leave behind)*	dejar
when does it leave?	*¿a qué hora sale?*
leek	el puerro
left: *on/to the left*	*a la izquierda*
left-luggage (office)	la consigna
leg	la pierna
legend	la leyenda
lemon	el limón
lemonade	la gaseosa
lemon tea	el té con limón
lend	prestar
length	la longitud
lens *(photographic)*	el objetivo
less	menos
lesson	la clase
let *(allow)*	permitir
(hire out)	alquilar
letter	la carta
(of alphabet)	la letra
letterbox	el buzón
lettuce	la lechuga
level crossing	el paso a nivel
library	la biblioteca
licence	el permiso
lid	la tapa
lie *(untruth)*	la mentira
lie down	tumbarse ; acostarse
life	la vida
lifeboat	el bote salvavidas
lifeguard	el/la socorrista
life jacket	el chaleco salvavidas

lift	el ascensor
lift pass (on ski slopes)	el "forfait"
light n	la luz
have you a light?	*¿tiene fuego?*
light vb	encender
light bulb	la bombilla
lighter	el encendedor
lightning	el relámpago
like prep	como
like you	*como tú*
like this	*así*
like vb	gustar
I like coffee	*me gusta el café*
lime (fruit)	la lima
line (row, queue)	la fila
(telephone)	la línea
lip salve	la crema protectora para labios
lipstick	la barra de labios
liqueur	el licor
list	la lista
listen (to)	escuchar
litre	el litro
litter	la basura
little	pequeño(a)
a little milk	*un poco de leche*
live	vivir
I live in Edinburgh	*vivo en Edimburgo*
liver	el hígado
living room	el cuarto de estar
loaf	la barra de pan
lobster	la langosta
local (wine, speciality)	de la región
lock vb (door)	cerrar con llave
lock n (on door, box)	la cerradura

locker *(luggage)*	la consigna automática
lollipop	la piruleta
London	Londres
long	largo(a)
for a long time	*(por) mucho tiempo*
look at	mirar
look after	cuidar
look for	buscar
lorry	el camión
lose	perder
lost *(object)*	perdido(a)
I've lost my wallet	*he perdido la cartera*
I'm lost	*me he perdido*
lost property office	la oficina de objetos perdidos
lot	mucho
lotion	la loción
loud *(sound, voice)*	fuerte
(volume)	alto(a)
lounge *(in hotel)*	el salón
love *n*	el amor
love *vb (person)*	querer
I love swimming	*me encanta nadar*
lovely	precioso(a)
low	bajo(a)
low tide	la marea baja
lucky: to be lucky	*tener suerte*
luggage	el equipaje
luggage allowance	la franquicia de equipaje
luggage rack *(car)*	la baca ; el portaequipajes
luggage tag	la etiqueta
luggage trolley	el carrito para el equipaje
lunch	el almuerzo ; la comida
luxury	de lujo

macaroni	los macarrones
machine	la máquina
mackerel	la caballa
mad	loco(a)
magazine	la revista
maid *(in hotel)*	la camarera
maiden name	el apellido de soltera
main	principal
main course	el plato principal
mains *(electric)*	la red eléctrica
Majorca	Mallorca
make *n (brand)*	la marca
make *vb (generally)*	hacer *see* GRAMMAR
(meal)	preparar
make-up	el maquillaje
male	masculino(a)
man	el hombre
manager	el/la gerente
managing director	el/la director(a) gerente
manufacture *vb*	fabricar
many	muchos(as)
map *(of region)*	el mapa
(of town)	el plano
marble	el mármol
margarine	la margarina
mark *(stain)*	la mancha
market	el mercado
marmalade	la mermelada de naranja
married	casado(a)
marry *(get married to)*	casarse con
marzipan	el mazapán
mass *(in church)*	la misa
mast	el mástil

match (game)	el partido
matches	las cerillas
material (cloth)	la tela
matter	importar ; pasar
it doesn't matter	no importa
what's the matter?	¿qué pasa?
mayonnaise	la mayonesa
meadow	el prado
meal	la comida
mean (signify)	querer decir
what does this mean?	¿qué quiere decir esto?
means	el medio ; el modo
measles	el sarampión
measure vb	medir
meat	la carne
mechanic	el/la mecánico
medicine	la medicina
medium	mediano(a)
medium rare	medio(a) hecho(a)
meet (by chance)	encontrarse con
(for first time)	conocer
(by arrangement)	reunirse con
meeting	la reunión
melon	el melón
melt	derretir
member (of club, etc.)	el/la socio(a)
men	los hombres
menu	la carta
meringue	el merengue
message	el mensaje ; el recado
metal	el metal
meter	el contador
metre	el metro
midday	el mediodía

midnight	la medianoche
migraine	la jaqueca
mile	la milla ; *5 miles = approx. 8 km*
milk	la leche
milkshake	el batido *[Lat. Am. la malteada]*
millimetre	el milímetro
million	el millón
mince	la carne picada
mind: *do you mind?*	¿le importa?
mineral water	el agua mineral
minimum	el mínimo
minister *(political)*	el ministro
minor road	la carretera secundaria
mint *(herb)*	la menta
(sweet)	la pastilla de menta
minute	el minuto
mirror	el espejo
miss *(train, etc.)*	perder
Miss	la señorita
missing *(thing)*	perdido(a)
my son is missing	se ha perdido mi hijo
mistake	el error
misty: *it's misty*	hay neblina
misunderstanding	la equivocación
there's been a misunderstanding	ha habido una equivocación
mix	mezclar
mixture	la mezcla
modern	moderno(a)
moisturizer	la leche hidratante
monastery	el monasterio
money	el dinero *[Lat. Am. la plata]*
monkey	el mono
month	el mes

monument	el monumento
moon	la luna
mop *n (for floor)*	la fregona
more	más
more wine, please	*más vino, por favor*
morning	la mañana
mosquito	el mosquito
most: *most of*	*la mayor parte de*
moth	la mariposa nocturna
(clothes)	la polilla
mother	la madre
mother-in-law	la suegra
motor	el motor
motor boat	la lancha motora
motor cycle	la motocicleta
motorway	la autopista
mountain	la montaña
mouse	el ratón
moustache	el bigote
mouth	la boca
move: *it isn't moving*	*no se mueve*
Mr	el señor (Sr.)
Mrs	la señora (Sra.)
much	mucho
it costs too much	*cuesta demasiado*
mud	el barro
mumps	las paperas
muscle	el músculo
museum	el museo
mushroom	el champiñon
music	la música
mussel	el mejillón
mustard	la mostaza
mutton	el cordero

nail *(fingernail)*	la uña
(metal)	el clavo
naked	desnudo(a)
name	el nombre
napkin	la servilleta
nappy	el pañal
narrow	estrecho(a)
nationality	la nacionalidad
navy blue	azul marino
near	cerca
necessary	necesario(a)
neck	el cuello
necklace	el collar
need	necesitar
I need an aspirin	*necesito una aspirina*
needle	la aguja
needle and thread	*aguja e hilo*
negative *(photography)*	el negativo
neighbour	el/la vecino(a)
nephew	el sobrino
nervous	nervioso(a)
nest	el nido
never	nunca
I never drink wine	*nunca bebo vino*
new	nuevo(a)
news	las noticias
newsagent	el vendedor de periódicos
newspaper	el periódico
New Year	el Año Nuevo
New Zealand	Nueva Zelanda
next: *the next stop*	la próxima parada
next week	la semana próxima
nice *(person)*	simpático(a)
(place, holiday)	bonito(a) *[lat Am linda(a)]*

niece	la sobrina
night	la noche
night club	el club nocturno
nightdress	el camisón
no	no
nobody	nadie
noisy	ruidoso(a)
nonalcoholic	sin alcohol
none	ninguno(a)
non-smoking *(on train)*	no fumador
north	el norte
Northern Ireland	Irlanda del Norte
nose	la nariz
not	no
I don't know	*no sé*
note *(bank note)*	el billete (de banco)
(letter)	la nota
note pad	el bloc
nothing	nada
nothing else	*nada más*
notice *(sign)*	el anuncio
(warning)	el aviso
novel	la novela
November	noviembre
now	ahora
number	el número
number plate	la matrícula
nurse	la enfermera
nursery school	la guardería infantil
nursery slope	la pista para principiantes
nut *(to eat)*	la nuez
(for bolt)	la tuerca
nutmeg	la nuez moscada
nuts *(in general)*	los frutos secos

oak	el roble
oar	el remo
oats	la avena
obvious	evidente
occasionally	de vez en cuando
octopus	el pulpo
odd	raro(a)
of	de
off *(machine, etc.)*	apagado(a)
this milk is off	*esta leche está pasada*
offence *(crime)*	el delito
(traffic)	la infracción
offer	ofrecer
office	la oficina
often	a menudo
oil	el aceite
oil filter	el filtro de aceite
ointment	el ungüento ; la pomada
OK *(agreed)*	vale
old	viejo(a)
how old are you?	*¿cuántos años tiene?*
olive oil	el aceite de oliva
olives	la aceitunas
olive tree	el olivo
omelette	la tortilla
on *(light, TV)*	encendido(a)
(tap)	abierto(a)
on the table	*sobre la mesa*
once	una vez
at once	en seguida
one	uno(a)
one-way *(street)*	(la calle de) dirección única
onion	la cebolla
only	sólo

open adj	abierto(a)
open vb	abrir
opera	la ópera
operator	el/la telefonista
opinion	la opinión
in my opinion	*en mi opinión*
opposite (to)	enfrente (de)
opposite the hotel	*enfrente del hotel*
or	o
orange adj	color naranja
orange n	la naranja
orange juice	el zumo de naranja
orchard	el huerto ; la huerta
order n	la orden
order vb	pedir ; ordenar
organize	organizar
other: *the other one*	el/la otro(a)
have you any others?	*¿tiene otros?*
ounce	la onza = *approx. 30 g*
out (light)	apagado(a)
he's out	*ha salido*
outdoor (pool, etc.)	al aire libre
outside	fuera
outskirts	las afueras
oven	el horno
over (on top of)	(por) encima de
overcharge	cobrar demasiado
overcoat	el abrigo
overnight (travel)	por la noche
owe	deber
I owe you ...	*le debo ...*
owner	el/la propietario(a)
oxygen	el oxígeno
oyster	la ostra

pack *(luggage)*	hacer las maletas
package tour	el viaje organizado
packed lunch	el almuerzo frío
packet	el paquete
padlock	el candado
page	la página
paid	pagado(a)
painful	doloroso(a)
painkiller	el analgésico
painting	la pintura
pair	el par
palace	el palacio
pale	pálido(a)
pan	la cacerola
pancake	el crep(e)
panties	las bragas
pants *(men's underwear)*	los calzoncillos
paper	el papel
paraffin	la parafina
parcel	el paquete
pardon?	¿cómo?
parents	los padres
park *n*	el parque
park *vb*	aparcar
parking disk	el disco de estacionamiento
parsley	el perejil
part	la parte
party *(group)*	el grupo
(celebration)	la fiesta
passenger	el/la pasajero(a)
passport	el pasaporte
passport control	el control de pasaportes
pasta	la pasta

pastry (dough)	la masa
(cake)	el pastel
pâté	el paté
path	el camino
pavement	la acera
pay	pagar
payment	el pago
peach	el melocotón
peanut	el cacahuete
pear	la pera
peas	los guisantes
pebble	el guijarro
pedestrian	el peatón
peel (fruit)	pelar
peg (for clothes)	la pinza
(for tent)	el gancho
pen	el bolígrafo ; la pluma
pencil	el lápiz
penicillin	la penicilina
penknife	la navaja
pensioner	el/la jubilado(a)
pepper (spice)	la pimienta
(vegetable)	el pimiento
per: per hour	por hora
per week	a la semana
perfect	perfecto(a)
performance	la representación
(musical)	la actuación
perfume	el perfume
period (menstruation)	la regla
perm	la permanente
permit	el permiso
person	la persona
petrol	la gasolina

petrol station	la estación de servicio ; la gasolinera
phone	see telephone
photocopy n	la fotocopia
photocopy vb	fotocopiar
photograph	la fotografía
pickle	el encurtido
picnic	el "picnic"
picture (painting)	el cuadro
(photo)	la foto
pie (fruit)	la tarta
(meat)	el pastel de carne
(and/or vegetable)	la empanada
piece	el pedazo
pill	la píldora
pillow	la almohada
pillowcase	la funda
pin	el alfiler
pineapple	la piña
pink	rosa
pint	la pinta = approx. 0.5 litre
a pint of beer	una cerveza grande
pipe (smoker's)	la pipa
plaster (for small cuts)	la tirita®
plastic	el plástico
plate	el plato
platform	el andén ; la vía
play (games)	jugar
playroom	el cuarto de jugar
please	por favor
pleased	contento(a)
pliers	los alicates
plug (electrical)	el enchufe
(for sink)	el tapón

plum	la ciruela
plumber	el fontanero
points (in car)	los platinos
poisonous	venenoso(a)
police	la policía
police!	¡policía!
policeman	el policía
police station	la comisaría de policía
polish (for shoes)	el betún
polluted	contaminado(a)
pony-trekking	la excursión a caballo
pool (swimming)	la piscina
pork	el cerdo
port (seaport)	el puerto
(wine)	el oporto
porter	el mozo
portrait	el retrato
Portugal	Portugal
Portuguese	portugués/portuguesa
possible	posible
post vb	echar
postbox	el buzón
postcard	la postal
postcode	el código postal
post office	la oficina de correos
pot (for cooking)	la olla
potato	la patata
pottery	la cerámica
pound (weight)	= approx. 0.5 kilo
pound (money)	la libra
pour	echar
powdered milk	la leche en polvo
prawn	la gamba
prefer	preferir

pregnant	embarazada
prepare	preparar
prescription	la receta médica
present *(gift)*	el regalo
pretty	bonito(a)
price	el precio
price list	la lista de precios
priest	el sacerdote
prince	el príncipe
princess	la princesa
private	privado(a)
prize	el premio
problem	el problema
producer *(TV, film)*	el/la realizador(a)
programme	el programa
prohibited	prohibido(a)
pronounce	pronunciar
how's it pronounced?	¿cómo se pronuncia?
Protestant	protestante
prune	la ciruela pasa
public	público(a)
public holiday	el día festivo
pudding	el postre
pull	tirar
pullover	el jersey
puncture	el pinchazo
purple	morado(a)
purse	el monedero
push	empujar
pushchair	la silla de niño
put	poner
pyjamas	el pijama
Pyrenees	los Pirineos

quality	la calidad
quarrel vb	reñir
quay	el muelle
queen	la reina
question	la pregunta
queue n	la cola
queue vb	hacer cola
quick	rápido(a)
quickly	de prisa
quiet (place)	tranquilo(a)
quilt	el edredón
quite: it's quite good	es bastante bueno
quite expensive	bastante caro

rabbit	el conejo
rabies	la rabia
race	la carrera
rack (luggage)	la rejilla
racket (tennis)	la raqueta
radio	la radio
radishes	los rábanos
railway	el ferrocarril
railway station	la estación de ferrocarril
rain	la lluvia
raincoat	el impermeable
raining: it's raining	está lloviendo
raisin	la pasa
ramp	la rampa
rare (unique)	excepcional
(steak)	poco hecho(a)
rash (skin)	el sarpullido
raspberry	la frambuesa
rat	la rata

rate	la tarifa
rate of exchange	*el tipo de cambio*
raw	crudo(a)
razor	la maquinilla de afeitar
razor blades	las hojas de afeitar
read	leer
ready	listo(a)
to get ready	*prepararse*
real	auténtico(a) ; verdadero(a)
realise	darse cuenta de
reason	la razón
receipt	el recibo
recently	recientemente
reception (desk)	la recepción
recipe	la receta
recognize	reconocer
recommend	recomendar
record *(music, etc.)*	el disco
red	rojo(a)
redcurrant	la grosella roja
reduction	el descuento
reel	el carrete
refill *(for pen)*	el recambio
refund *vb*	devolver el importe
registered	certificado(a)
regulation	la norma ; el reglamento
reimburse	reembolsar
relation *(family)*	el familiar ; el pariente
relax	relajarse
reliable *(method)*	seguro(a)
remain	permanecer ; quedarse
remember	recordar
rent	alquilar

rental	el alquiler
repair	reparar
repeat	repetir
reservation	la reserva
reserve	reservar
reserved	reservado(a)
rest n *(repose)*	el descanso
the rest of the wine	*el resto del vino*
rest *vb*	descansar
restaurant	el restaurante
restaurant car	el coche-restaurante
retire	jubilarse
return *(go back)*	volver
(give back)	devolver
return ticket	el billete de ida y vuelta
reverse charge call	la llamada a cobro revertido
rheumatism	el reumatismo
rhubarb	el ruibarbo
rice	el arroz
rich *(person, etc.)*	rico(a)
(food)	pesado(a)
riding	la equitación
I like riding	*me gusta montar a caballo*
right *adj (correct)*	correcto(a)
to be right	*tener razón*
right: on/to the right	a la derecha
ring	el anillo
ripe	maduro(a)
river	el río
road	la carretera
road conditions	el estado de las carreteras
road map	el mapa de carreteras
road works	las obras
roast	asado(a)

rob	robar
robber	el ladrón
roll *(bread)*	el panecillo ; el bollo
roof	el tejado
roof-rack	la baca
room *(in house, hotel)*	el cuarto ; la habitación
(space)	sitio
room service	el servicio de habitaciones
rope	la cuerda
rose	la rosa
rosé	el rosado
rotten *(fruit, etc.)*	podrido(a)
rough *(sea)*	picado(a)
round *(shape)*	redondo(a)
roundabout *(traffic)*	la plaza circular ; la glorieta
route	la ruta
row n *(line)*	la fila
row vb *(boat)*	remar
rowing boat	la barca de remos
royal	real
rubber *(material)*	la goma
(eraser)	la goma de borrar
rubber band	la gomita
rubbish	la basura
rucksack	la mochila
rudder	el timón
rug	la alfombra
ruins	las ruinas
ruler *(measuring)*	la regla
rum	el ron
run *(skiing)*	la pista
rush hour	la hora punta
rusty	oxidado(a)
rye bread	el pan de centeno

sad	triste
safe *n*	la caja fuerte
safe *adj*	seguro(a) ; sin peligro
safety pin	el imperdible
sail	la vela
sailboard	la tabla de "windsurf"
sailing *(sport)*	la vela
saint/saint's day	el santo
salad	la ensalada
salad dressing	el aliño
sale	la rebaja ; la liquidación
salesperson	el/la vendedor(a)
salmon	el salmón
salt	la sal
same	mismo(a)
sample	la muestra
sand	la arena
sandals	las sandalias
sandwich *(French bread)*	el bocadillo
(toasted)	el "sandwich"
sanitary towels	las compresas
sardine	la sardina
sauce	la salsa
saucepan	la cacerola
saucer	el platillo
sauna	la sauna
sausage	la salchicha
save	salvar
(money)	ahorrar
savoury *(not sweet)*	salado(a)
say	decir
scallop	la vieira
scampi	las gambas

scarf (woollen)	la bufanda
(silk)	el pañuelo
school	la escuela
scissors	las tijeras
score n	la puntuación
score vb (goal)	marcar
Scotch	el whisky escocés
Scotland	Escocia
Scottish	escocés/escocesa
screw	el tornillo
screwdriver	el destornillador
sculpture (object)	la escultura
sea	el mar
seafood	los mariscos
seasick	mareado(a)
seaside: at the seaside	en la playa
season ticket	el abono
seat (chair)	la silla
(in bus, train)	el asiento
second	segundo(a)
second class	de segunda clase
see	ver
seem: it seems to me	me parece
self-service	el autoservicio
sell	vender
Sellotape®	el celo
send	enviar
senior citizen	el/la pensionista
separate	separado(a)
serious (accident, etc.)	grave
(person)	serio(a)
serve	servir
service (in restaurant)	el servicio
service charge	el servicio

set menu	el menú del día
set off *vb*	partir
several	varios(as)
sew	coser
shade	la sombra
shallow	poco profundo(a)
shampoo	el champú
shampoo and set	lavar y marcar
shandy	la cerveza con gaseosa
share	repartir
shave	afeitarse
shaving cream	la crema de afeitar
she	ella *see* GRAMMAR
sheep	la oveja
sheet	la sábana
shellfish	los mariscos
sherry	el jerez
ship	el barco
shirt	la camisa
shock	el susto
shock absorber	el amortiguador
shoe	el zapato
shoot	disparar
shop	la tienda
shop assistant	el/la dependiente(a)
shopping	las compras
to go shopping	*ir de compras*
short	corto(a)
short cut	el atajo
shorts	los pantalones cortos
shout	el grito
show *n*	el espectáculo
show *vb*	enseñar

shower	la ducha *[Mexico* la regadera*]*
shrimp	el camarón
shut *adj*	cerrado(a)
shut *vb*	cerrar
sick *(ill)*	enfermo(a)
side	el lado
sightseeing	la excursión turística
sign *n (road sign)*	la señal
sign *vb*	firmar
signature	la firma
silence	el silencio
silk	la seda
silly	tonto(a)
silver	la plata
similar	parecido(a)
simple	sencillo(a)
sing	cantar
single *(unmarried)*	soltero(a)
(not double)	sencillo(a)
single bed	la cama individual
single room	la habitación individual
sink	el fregadero
sir	señor
sister	la hermana
sit	sentarse
size *(of clothing)*	la talla
skates	los patines
skating	el patinaje
ski *n*	el esquí
ski *vb*	esquiar
ski boot	la bota de esquí
skiing	el esquí
skimmed milk	la leche desnatada

skin	la piel
skindiving	el submarinismo
ski pants	los pantalones de esquí
ski pole	el bastón de esquí
skirt	la falda
ski run	la pista de esquí
ski suit	el traje de esquí
sky	el cielo
sledge	el trineo
sleep	dormir
sleeper *(in train)*	la litera
sleeping bag	el saco de dormir
sleeping car	el coche-cama ; la litera
sleeping pill	el somnífero
slice *(of bread)*	la rebanada
(of ham)	la loncha
slide *(photograph)*	la diapositiva
slipper	la zapatilla
slow	lento(a)
slowly	despacio
small	pequeño(a)
smaller	más pequeño(a)
smell *n*	el olor
smell *vb*	oler
it smells bad!	¡huele mal!
smile *n*	la sonrisa
smile *vb*	sonreír
smoke *n*	el humo
smoke *vb*	fumar
smoked	ahumado(a)
snack bar	la cafetería
snorkel	el tubo
snow *n*	la nieve
snow *vb*	nevar

snowing: *it's snowing*	está nevando
so: *so much*	tanto(a)
soap	el jabón
soap powder	el jabón en polvo
sober	sobrio(a)
socket	el enchufe
socks	los calcetines
soda	la soda
soft *(not hard)*	blando(a)
(smooth)	suave
soft drink	la bebida sin alcohol ; el refresco
some	algunos(as)
someone	alguien
something	algo
sometimes	a veces
son	el hijo
song	la canción
soon	pronto
sore: *it's sore*	duele
my back is sore	me duele la espalda
sorry: *sorry!*	¡perdón!
I'm sorry!	¡lo siento!
sort: *what sort of car?*	¿qué clase de coche?
soup	la sopa
south	el sur
souvenir	el recuerdo
space: *parking space*	el sitio para aparcar
spade	la pala
Spain	España
Spanish	español(a)
spanner	la llave inglesa
spare wheel	la rueda de repuesto/recambio
sparkling	espumoso(a)
spark plug	la bujía

speak	hablar
special	especial
speciality	la especialidad
speed	la velocidad
speed limit	la velocidad máxima
spell: *how is it spelt?*	¿cómo se escribe?
spicy	picante
spinach	las espinacas
spirits	el alcohol
spit *vb*	escupir
sponge	la esponja
spoon	la cuchara
sport	el deporte
spring *(season)*	la primavera
square *(in town)*	la plaza
squash *(game)*	el squash
(orange/lemon drink)	la naranjada/la limonada
squid	el calamar
stairs	las escaleras
stalls *(theatre)*	las butacas de patio
stamp *(postage)*	el sello
star	la estrella
start *(car)*	poner en marcha
starter *(in meal)*	entrada
(in car)	la puesta en marcha
station	la estación
stationer's	la papelería
stay *(remain)*	quedarse
I'm staying at hotel...	*me quedo en el hotel...*
steak	el filete
steep: *is it steep?*	¿hay mucha subida?
sterling *(pounds)*	las libras esterlinas
stew	el estofado
steward *(on plane)*	el auxiliar de vuelo

stewardess *(on plane)*	la azafata
sticking plaster	el esparadrapo
still *adv*	todavía
sting *n*	la picadura
sting *vb*	picar
stockings	las medias
stomach	el estómago
stomach upset	el trastorno estomacal
stone	la piedra
stop	parar
stopover	la escala
storey	el piso
storm	la tormenta
(at sea)	el temporal
straight on	todo recto [Lat. Am. derecho]
strainer	el colador
straw *(for drinking)*	la pajita
strawberry	la fresa
street	la calle
street map	el plano de la ciudad
string	la cuerda
striped	a rayas
strong	fuerte
stuck: *it's stuck*	*está atascado(a)*
student	el/la estudiante
stung	picado(a)
stupid	tonto(a)
success	el éxito
suddenly	de repente
suede	el ante
sugar	el azúcar
suit *n*	el traje
suit: *it doesn't suit me*	*no me sienta bien*

suitcase	la maleta
summer	el verano
sun	el sol
sunbathe	tomar el sol
sunburn	la quemadura del sol
sunglasses	las gafas de sol
sunny: *it's sunny*	*hace sol*
sunshade	la sombrilla
sunstroke	la insolación
suntan	el bronceado
suntan lotion	el bronceador
supermarket	el supermercado
supplement	el suplemento
sure	seguro(a)
surfboard	la tabla de "surf"
surname	el apellido
surprise	la sorpresa
surrounded by	rodeado(a) de
swallow *vb*	tragarse
sweat	el sudor
sweater	el suéter
sweet	el dulce
sweetener	el edulcorante
sweets	los caramelos
swim	nadar
swimming pool	la piscina
swimsuit	el traje de baño
swing *(seat)*	el columpio
switch	el interruptor
switch off *(engine)*	parar
switch on	encender
swollen	hinchado(a)
synagogue	la sinagoga

table	la mesa
tablecloth	el mantel
tablespoon	la cuchara
tablet	la pastilla
table wine	el vino de mesa
tail	la cola
tailor's	la sastrería
take *(medicine, etc.)*	tomar
how long does it take?	¿cuánto tiempo se tarda?
take out	sacar
talc	los polvos de talco
talk	hablar
tall	alto(a)
tame	manso(a)
tampons	los tampones
tap	el grifo *[Lat. Am. la llave]*
tape	la cinta
tape-recorder	el magnetofón
tartar sauce	la salsa tártara
taste *vb : can I taste it?*	¿puedo probarlo?
taste *n*	el sabor
tax	el impuesto
taxi	el taxi
taxi driver	el/la taxista
taxi rank	la parada de taxis
tea	el té
teabag	la bolsita de té
teach	enseñar
teacher	el/la profesor(a)
team	el equipo
teapot	la tetera
tear *(crying)*	la lágrima
(in material)	el rasgón
teaspoon	la cucharilla

teat *(on baby's bottle)*	la tetina
teeshirt	la camiseta
teeth	los dientes
telegram	el telegrama
telephone	el teléfono
telephone box	la cabina telefónica
telephone call	la llamada telefónica
telephone directory	la guía telefónica
television	la televisión
telex	el télex
tell	decir
I will tell him	*se lo diré*
temperature	la temperatura
I have a temperature	*tengo fiebre*
temporary	provisional
tennis	el tenis
tennis ball	la pelota de tenis
tennis court	la pista de tenis
tennis racket	la raqueta de tenis
tent	la tienda de campaña
tent peg	el gancho
terminus	la (estación) terminal
terrace	la terraza
text	el texto
than	que
more than	*más que*
less than	*menos que*
thank you	gracias
thanks very much	*muchas gracias*
that	eso ; aquello
that book	*ese libro*
that table	*esa mesa*
that one	*ése/ésa*
thaw	el deshielo
theatre	el teatro

T

then	entonces
(afterwards)	luego
there	allí
there is/there are	hay
therefore	por lo tanto
thermometer	el termómetro
these	estos/estas
they	ellos/ellas *see* GRAMMAR
thick	grueso(a)
thief	el ladrón/la ladrona
thigh	el muslo
thin	delgado(a)
thing	la cosa
my things	mis cosas
think	pensar
(be of opinion)	creer
third	tercero(a)
thirsty: *I'm thirsty*	tengo sed
this	esto ; este/esta
those	esos/esas
thread	el hilo
throat	la garganta
throat lozenge	la pastilla para la garganta
through	por
thunder	el trueno
thunderstorm	la tormenta
ticket	el billete *[Lat. Am. el boleto]*
ticket collector	el/la revisor(a)
ticket office	el despacho de billetes
tide	la marea
tie	la corbata
tights	las medias
till *n*	la caja
till *prep*	hasta

time	el tiempo
for the first time	*por primera vez*
this time	*esta vez*
what time is it?	*¿qué hora es?*
timetable	el horario
tin	la lata
tinfoil	el papel de aluminio
tin-opener	el abrelatas
tip *n (to waiter, etc.)*	la propina
tipped	con filtro
tired	cansado(a)
tissues	los pañuelos de papel
to	a
toast	el pan tostado ; la tostada
tobacco	el tabaco
tobacconist's	el estanco
today	hoy
a week today	*de hoy en ocho días*
together	juntos(as)
toilet	los aseos ; los servicios
toilet paper	el papel higiénico
toll	el peaje
tomato	el tomate
tomato juice	el zumo de tomate
tomorrow	mañana
tomorrow morning	*mañana por la mañana*
tomorrow afternoon	*mañana por la tarde*
tongue	la lengua
tonic water	la tónica
tonight	esta noche
too *(also)*	también
too big	*demasiado grande*
too small	*demasiado pequeño(a)*
tooth	el diente
toothache	el dolor de muelas

toothbrush	el cepillo de dientes
toothpaste	la pasta de dientes
toothpick	el palillo
top adj : the top floor	el último piso
top n (of hill)	la cima
on top of …	sobre …
torch	la linterna
torn	rasgado(a)
total	el total
tough (meat)	duro(a)
tour (trip)	la vuelta
(of museum, etc.)	la visita
tourist	el/la turista
tourist office	la oficina de turismo
tourist ticket	el billete turístico
tow	remolcar
towel	la toalla
tower	la torre
town	la ciudad
town centre	el centro de la ciudad
town hall	el ayuntamiento
town plan	el plano de la ciudad
tow rope	el cable de remolque
toy	el juguete
traditional	tradicional
traffic	la circulación ; el tráfico
traffic lights	el semáforo
trailer	el remolque
train	el tren
by train	en tren
training shoes	las zapatillas de deporte
tram	el tranvía
translate	traducir
translation	la traducción

travel	viajar
travel agent	el agente de viajes
traveller's cheque	el cheque de viaje
tray	la bandeja
tree	el árbol
trip	la excursión ; el viaje
trolley	el carrito
trouble	el problema
trousers	los pantalones
trout	la trucha
true	verdadero(a)
trunk (luggage)	el baúl
trunks	el bañador
truth	la verdad
try (attempt)	intentar
try on (clothes)	probarse
tuna	el bonito ; el atún
tunnel	el túnel
turkey	el pavo
turn	girar
turn left	gire a la izquierda
turnip	el nabo
turn off (light, etc.)	apagar
(tap)	cerrar
(engine)	parar
turn on (light, etc.)	encender
(tap)	abrir
tweezers	las pinzas
twice	dos veces
twin-bedded room	la habitación con dos camas
type vb	escribir a máquina
typical	típico(a)
tyre	el neumático
tyre pressure	la presión de los neumáticos

umbrella	el paraguas
uncle	el tío
uncomfortable	incómodo(a)
unconscious	inconsciente
under	debajo de
underground *(metro)*	el metro
underpants	los calzoncillos
underpass	el paso subterráneo
understand	entender
I don't understand	*no entiendo*
underwear	la ropa interior
unemployed	parado(a) ; desempleado(a)
unfasten	desabrocharse
unhappy with	descontento(a) con
United States	los Estados Unidos
university	la universidad
unleaded petrol	la gasolina sin plomo
unpack	deshacer las maletas
I have to unpack	*tengo que deshacer las maletas*
unscrew	destornillar
up	arriba
(out of bed)	levantado(a)
upside down	al revés
upstairs	arriba
urgent	urgente
urine	la orina
USA	EE. UU.
use	usar
used to: *I'm used to…*	estoy acostumbrado(a) a…
useful	útil
usual	normal ; corriente
the usual	*lo de siempre*
usually	por lo general
U-turn	el cambio de sentido

vacancy *(in hotel)*	la habitación libre
vacuum cleaner	la aspiradora
valid	válido(a)
valley	el valle
valuable	de valor
valuables	los objetos de valor
van	la furgoneta ; la camioneta
vase	el florero
VAT	el IVA
veal	la ternera
vegetables	las verduras
vegetarian	vegetariano(a)
vein	la vena
velvet	el terciopelo
ventilator	el ventilador
vermouth	el vermú
very	muy
vest	la camiseta
via	por
video	el vídeo
video camera	la vídeo-cámara
view	la vista
villa	la casa de campo ; el chalé
village	el pueblo
vinegar	el vinagre
vineyard	la viña ; el viñedo
visa	el visado
visit	la visita
vitamin	la vitamina
vodka	el vodka
voice	la voz
voltage	el voltaje

wage	el sueldo
waist	la cintura
wait for	esperar
waiter	el camarero
waiting room	la sala de espera
waitress	la camarera
Wales	el País de Gales
walk *vb*	andar ; pasear
walk *n*	un paseo
to go for a walk	*dar un paseo*
walking stick	el bastón
wall *(inside)*	la pared
(outside)	el muro
wallet	la cartera
walnut	la nuez
want	querer see GRAMMAR
war	la guerra
warm	caliente
it's warm (weather)	*hace calor*
warning triangle	el triángulo señalizador
wash	lavar
(wash oneself)	lavarse
washbasin	el lavabo
washing machine	la lavadora
washing powder	el jabón en polvo
washing-up liquid	el líquido lavavajillas
wasp	la avispa
waste *vb (money)*	malgastar
(time)	perder
waste bin	el cubo de la basura
watch *n*	el reloj
watch *vb (look at)*	mirar
watchstrap	la correa de reloj
water	el agua

waterfall	la cascada
water heater	el calentador de agua
watermelon	la sandía
waterproof	resistente al agua
water-skiing	el esquí acuático
wave *(on sea)*	la ola
wax	la cera
way *(manner)*	la manera
(route)	el camino
we	nosotros(as) *see* **GRAMMAR**
weak *(person)*	débil
(coffee)	flojo(a)
wear	llevar
weather	el tiempo
wedding	la boda
week	la semana
weekday	el día laborable
weekend	el fin de semana
weight	el peso
welcome	bienvenido(a)
well	bien
he's not well	*no está bien*
well done *(steak)*	muy hecho(a)
Welsh	galés/galesa
west	el oeste
wet	mojado(a)
(weather)	lluvioso(a)
wetsuit	el traje de bucear
what?	¿qué?
what is it?	*¿qué es?*
wheel	la rueda
wheelchair	la silla de ruedas
when	cuando
when?	*¿cuándo?*

where *conj.*	donde
where?	¿dónde?
which: *which is it?*	¿cuál es?
while	mientras
in a short while	dentro de un rato
whisky	el whisky
white	blanco(a)
who: *who is it?*	¿quién es?
whole	entero(a)
wholemeal bread	el pan integral
whose: *whose is it?*	¿de quién es?
why?	¿por qué?
wide	ancho(a)
wife	la mujer ; la esposa
window	la ventana
(shop)	el escaparate *[Lat. Am.* la vitrina]
(in car, train)	la ventanilla
windscreen	el parabrisas
windsurfing	el "windsurfing"
windy: *it's windy*	hace viento
wine	el vino
wine list	la carta de vinos
winter	el invierno
with	con
without	sin
woman	la mujer
wood *(material)*	la madera
(forest)	el bosque
wool	la lana
word	la palabra
work *(person)*	trabajar
(machine, car)	funcionar
worried	preocupado(a)
worse	peor

worth: *it's worth ...*	*vale ...*
wrap (up)	envolver
wrapping paper	el papel de envolver
write	escribir
writing paper	el papel de escribir
wrong *(incorrect)*	**equivocado(a)**
what's wrong	*¿qué pasa?*
X-ray	la radiografía
yacht	el yate
year	el año
yellow	amarillo(a)
yes	sí
yes, please	*sí, por favor*
yesterday	ayer
yet: *not yet*	*todavía no*
yoghurt	el yogur
you *(polite sing.)*	**usted** *see* **GRAMMAR**
(polite plural)	ustedes
(sing. with friends)	tú
(plural with friends)	vosotros
young	joven
youth hostel	el albergue juvenil
zero	el cero
zip	la cremallera
zoo	el zoo

a: a la estación	to the station
a las 4	at 4 o'clock
a 30 kilómetros	30 kilometres away
abadía f	abbey
abajo	below ; downstairs
hacia abajo	downward(s)
abeja f	bee
abierto(a)	open ; on (water supply)
abogado(a) m/f	lawyer
abonados mpl	season-ticket holders
abonar	to pay ; to credit
abono m	season ticket
abrir	to open ; to turn on (tap)
abrochar	to fasten
abuela f	grandmother
abuelo m	grandfather
acá	here
aburrido(a)	boring
acampar	to camp
acceso m	access
acceso andenes	to the platforms
acceso prohibido	no access
acceso vías	to the platforms
accidente m	accident
aceite m	oil
aceite bronceador	suntan oil
aceite de oliva	olive oil
aceituna f	olive
aceitunas aliñadas	seasoned olives
acelgas fpl	chard
acera f	pavement
acero m	steel
aconsejar	to advise
acto m	act
en el acto	while you wait (repairs, etc.)

actor *m*	actor
actriz *f*	actress
acuerdo *m*	agreement
¡de acuerdo!	OK ; alright
adiós	goodbye
administración *f*	administration ; management
admitir	to accept ; to permit
no se admiten...	...not permitted
adobado(a)	marinated in garlic, herbs, etc.
adolescente *m/f*	teenager
aduana *f*	customs
adulto(a)	adult
advertir	to warn
aerobús *m*	air bus
aerodeslizador *m*	hovercraft
aerolínea *f*	airline
aeropuerto *m*	airport
afeitarse	to shave
afiche *m*	poster ; sign *(Lat. Am.)*
agarrar	to take ; to catch *(bus, etc. Lat. Am.)*
agencia *f*	agency
agencia de seguros	insurance company
agencia de viajes	travel agency
agente *m/f*	agent
agente de policía	policeman ; policewoman
agitar: agítese	shake well *(on bottles)*
agosto *m*	August
agotado(a)	sold out ; out of stock
agradecer	to thank
agridulce	sweet and sour
agua *f*	water
agua destilada	distilled water
agua del grifo	tap water
agua potable	drinking water
agua de selta	soda water

aguacate m	avocado
agudo(a)	sharp ; pointed
aguja f	needle ; hand (watch)
agujero m	hole
ahogarse	to drown
ahumado(a)	smoked
aire m	air
al aire libre	open-air ; outdoor
aire acondicionado m	air-conditioning
ajete m	young garlic
ajillo: al ajillo	in a garlic sauce
ajo m	garlic
ajo blanco	cold almond and garlic soup
ala f	wing
a la carta	à la carte (menu)
alarma f	alarm
alarma de incendios	fire alarm
albahaca f	basil
albaricoque m	apricot
albarán m	delivery note
albergue m	hostel
albergue juvenil	youth hostel
albóndiga f	meatball
alcachofa f	artichoke
alcance m	reach
alcanzar	to reach ; to get ; to catch up
alcaparras fpl	capers
alcohol m	alcohol
alérgico(a) a	allergic to
aletas fpl	flippers
alfarería f	pottery
alfombra f	carpet
algas fpl	seaweed
algo	something

algodón *m*	cotton
algodón hidrófilo	cotton wool
alimentación *f*	grocery shop ; food
alimento *m*	food
alioli *m*	garlic-flavoured mayonnaise
alitas de pollo *fpl*	chicken wings
all i oli *m*	garlic-flavoured mayonnaise
almacén *m*	store
grandes almacenes	department stores
almeja *f*	clam ; mussel
almendra *f*	almond
almíbar *m*	syrup
almuerzo *m*	lunch
alojamiento *m*	accommodation
alquilar	to rent ; to hire
se alquila	to let
alquiler *m*	rent ; rental
alto(a)	high ; tall
alta tensión	high voltage
altura *f*	altitude ; height
alubias blancas *fpl*	butter beans
alubias pintas *fpl*	red kidney beans
amable	pleasant ; kind
amargo(a)	bitter
amarillo(a)	yellow
ambulancia *f*	ambulance
ambulatorio *m*	National Health clinic
ampolla *f*	blister
análisis *m*	analysis
análisis de sangre	blood test
ananá(s) *m*	pineapple
anchoa *f*	anchovy
anchura *f*	width
ancla *f*	anchor

andaluz(a)	**Andalusian**
andar	**to walk**
andén *m*	**platform** *(at train station)*
añejo(a)	**mature ; vintage**
anguila *f*	**eel**
anís *m*	**liqueur ; aniseed** *(seeds of plant)*
año *m*	**year**
Año Nuevo	**New Year's Day**
ante *m*	**suede**
anteojos *mpl*	**binoculars ; spectacles** *(Lat. Am.)*
antes	**before**
antibiótico *m*	**antibiotic**
anticonceptivo *m*	**contraceptive**
anticongelante *m*	**antifreeze**
antiguo(a)	**old**
antiséptico *m*	**antiseptic**
anular	**to cancel**
anunciar	**to announce ; to advertise**
apagado(a)	**off** *(switch)*
apagar	**to switch off ; to turn off**
aparato *m*	**appliance**
aparcamiento *m*	**parking-lot ; car park**
aparcar	**to park**
apartadero *m*	**lay-by**
apartado de Correos *m*	**PO Box**
apartamento *m*	**apartment**
apellido *m*	**surname**
apellido de soltera	**maiden name**
aperitivo *m*	**apéritif ; appetizer**
apertura *f*	**opening**
apio *m*	**celery**
aplazar	**to postpone**
apto(a)	**suitable**

aquí	here
arena *f*	sand
arenque *m*	herring
armario *m*	wardrobe ; cupboard
arrancar	to switch on
arriba	upstairs
hacia arriba	upward(s)
arroz *m*	rice
arroz abanda	seafood risotto
arroz blanco	plain boiled rice
arroz a la cubana	rice with egg and tomato sauce
arroz con leche	rice pudding
arte *f*	art
artesanía *f*	crafts
artículo *m*	article
artículos de tocador	toiletries
artículos de ocasión	bargains
asado(a)	roast
ascensor *m*	lift
asegurado(a)	insured
aseos *mpl*	toilets
asiento *m*	seat
asistencia *f*	help ; assistance
asistencia técnica	repairs
asma *f*	asthma
aspirador *m*	vacuum cleaner
aspirina *f*	aspirin
¡atención!	take care!
atrás	behind
ATS *m/f*	nurse
atún *m*	tuna fish
atún encebollado	tuna casserole
auricular *m*	receiver
auriculares *mpl*	headphones
autobús *m*	bus

autocar m	coach
automático(a)	automatic
autopista f	motorway
autoservicio m	self-service
auto-stop m	hitch-hiking
Av./Avda.	*abbrev. for* avenida
ave f	bird
aves de corral	poultry
avellana f	hazelnut
avenida f	avenue
avería f	breakdown
averiado(a)	out of order ; broken down
avión m	aircraft ; aeroplane
aviso m	notice ; warning
ayudar	to help
ayuntamiento m	town hall
azafata f	air hostess
azafrán m	saffron
azúcar m	sugar
azul	blue
día azul	cheaper day to travel by train
zona azul	controlled parking area
baca f	roof rack
bacalao m	cod
bahía f	bay
bailar	to dance
bajar	to go down ; to drop *(temperature)*
bajarse	to get off
bajo(a)	low ; short ; soft *(sound)*
más bajo	lower
balneario m	spa
balón m	ball

baloncesto m	basketball
banana f	banana
bañador m	swimming costume
bañarse	to go swimming ; to bathe
banca f	banking ; bank
banco m	bench ; bank
banda f	band (musical)
bandeja f	tray
bandera f	flag
bañista m/f	bather
baño m	bath ; bathroom
con baño	with bath
barato(a)	cheap
barbacoa f	barbecue
barca f	small boat
barco m	ship ; boat
barra f	bar ; counter ; bread stick
barrera f	barrier ; crash barrier
barrio m	district ; suburb
barrio chino	red light district
basura f	rubbish
batata f	sweet potato (Lat. Am.)
batido m	milkshake
baúl m	trunk
bebé m	baby
beber	to drink
bebida f	drink
béisbol m	baseball
berberecho m	cockle
berenjena f	aubergine
berza f	cabbage
besugo m	sea bream
betún m	polish
biberón m	baby's bottle

Spanish	English
biblioteca f	library
bicicleta f	bicycle
bien	well
bienvenido(a)	welcome
bifurcación f	fork (in road)
billar m	snooker
billete m	ticket
billete de banco	bank note
billetera f	wallet
bistec m	steak
bisutería f	costume jewellery
bizcocho m	spongecake
blanco(a)	white
dejar en blanco	leave blank (on form)
blando(a)	soft
boca f	mouth
bocadillo m	sandwich (made with French bread)
boda f	wedding
bodega f	wine cellar ; restaurant
boite f	night club
boleto m	ticket (Lat. Am.)
bolígrafo m	biro
bollo m	roll ; bun
bolsa f	bag ; stock exchange
bolsa de plástico	plastic bag
bolsillo m	pocket
bolso m	bag (handbag)
bombero m	fireman
bombilla f	light bulb
bombona de gas f	gas cylinder
bombonería f	confectioner's
bombones mpl	chocolates
boniato m	sweet potato
bonito(a)	pretty ; nice-looking

bonito *m*	type of tuna fish
bono *m*	voucher
bono-bús *m*	bus pass
boquerón *m*	anchovy
bordado(a)	embroidered
bordo: a bordo	onboard
borracho(a)	drunk
bosque *m*	forest ; wood
bota *f*	boot
bote *m*	tin ; can
botella *f*	bottle
brasa: a la brasa	barbecued
brazo *m*	arm
bricolaje *m*	do-it-yourself *(shop)*
briñones *fpl*	nectarines
británico(a)	British
bronceado(a)	sun-tanned
broncearse	to tan
bronquitis *f*	bronchitis
brújula *f*	compass
bucear	to dive
bueno(a)	good ; fine
¡buenos días!	good morning!
¡buenas tardes!	good afternoon/evening!
¡buenas noches!	good evening/night!
bufet *m*	buffet
bufet libre *m*	set-price buffet in restaurant
bujía *f*	sparking plug
buñuelo *m*	fritter
burro *m*	donkey
butacas *fpl*	stalls *(theatre)*
butano *m*	Calor gas®
butifarra *f*	Catalan sausage
buzón *m*	postbox

caballa *f*	mackerel
Caballeros *mpl*	Gentlemen ; Gents
caballo *m*	horse
montar a caballo	to go riding
cabello *m*	hair
cabeza *f*	head
cabina *f*	cabin
cabina telefónica *f*	phone box
cable *m*	wire ; cable
cabrito *m*	kid *(young goat)*
cabrito asado	roast kid
cacahuete *m*	peanut
cacao *m*	cocoa
cacerola *f*	saucepan
cachemira *f*	cashmere
cada	every ; each
cada uno (c/u)	each (one)
cadena *f*	chain
caducado(a)	out-of-date
caerse	to fall down
café *m*	café ; coffee
café cortado	small coffee with dash of milk
corto de café	milky coffee
café descafeinado	decaffeinated coffee
café exprés	espresso coffee
café en grano	coffee beans
café con hielo	iced coffee
café con leche	white coffee
café molido	ground coffee
café solo	black coffee
cafetería *f*	snack bar ; coffee house
caja *f*	box ; cashdesk
caja de ahorros	savings bank
caja fuerte	safe
cajero(a) *m/f*	teller ; cashier
cajero automático	cash dispenser

calabacín m	courgette
calabacines rellenos	stuffed courgettes
calabaza f	pumpkin
calamares mpl	squid
calamares rellenos	stuffed squid
calculadora f	calculator
caldereta f	stew (fish, lamb)
caldo m	stock ; consommé
caldo de verduras	clear vegetable soup
calefacción f	heating
calefacción central	central heating
calentador m	heater
calentador de agua	water heater
calentar	to heat
calidad f	quality
caliente	hot
calle f	street
callos mpl	tripe
calmante m	painkiller
calzada f	roadway
calzada deteriorada	uneven road surface
calzado m	footwear
calzados	shoe shop
calzoncillos mpl	underpants
cama f	bed
dos camas	twin beds
cama individual	single bed
cama de matrimonio	double bed
cámara f	camera
camarera f	waitress
camarero m	barman ; waiter
camarón m	shrimp
camarote m	cabin
cambiar	to change ; to exchange
cambio m	change ; exchange (rate) ; gear

caminar	to walk
camino *m*	path ; road
camino particular	private road
camión *m*	truck ; lorry ; bus *(Lat. Am.)*
camioneta *f*	van
camisa *f*	shirt
camisería *f*	shirt shop
camisón *m*	nightdress
campana *f*	bell
camping *m*	campsite
campo *m*	field ; countryside
campo de golf	golf course
caña *f*	cane
caña de cerveza	glass of beer
caña de pescar	fishing rod
canasto *m*	basket
cancelar	to cancel
cancha de tenis *f*	tennis court
candela *f*	candle
canela *f*	cinnamon
canelones *mpl*	cannelloni
cangrejo *m*	crab
cangrejo de río	crayfish
canguro *m*	kangaroo
canguro *m/f*	babysitter
cansado(a)	tired
cantante *m/f*	singer
capilla *f*	chapel
capitán *m*	captain
capó *m*	bonnet ; hood *(of car)*
cápsulas *fpl*	capsules
cara *f*	face
caracol *m*	snail
caramelo *m*	sweet ; caramel

caravana f	caravan
carbonada f	minced beef stew (Lat. Am.)
carburador m	carburettor
carburante m	fuel
cárcel f	prison
carga f	load ; cargo
cargar	to load
cargar en cuenta	to charge to account
cargo m	charge
a cargo del cliente	at the customer's expense
Caribe m	Caribbean
carnaval m	carnival
carne f	meat
carne asada	roast meat
carné de conducir m	driving licence
carné de identidad m	identity card
carnicería f	butcher's
caro(a)	dear ; expensive
carpa f	carp
carpintería f	carpenter's shop
carrera f	career ; profession
carreras de caballos	horse-racing
carretera f	road ; highway
carril m	lane (on road)
carrito m	trolley (for luggage)
carro m	car (Lat. Am.)
carta f	letter ; playing card ; menu
carta aérea	air mail letter
carta certificada	registered letter
carta verde	green card (car insurance)
carta de vinos	wine list
cartel m	poster
cartelera f	entertainments guide
cartera f	wallet ; bag
carterista m	pickpocket

casa f	home ; house ; household
casa de campo	farmhouse
casa de huéspedes	boarding house
casa de socorro	first-aid post
casado(a)	married
casco m	helmet
casero(a)	home-made
comida casera	home cooking
caseta f	beach hut
caso : en caso de	in case of
caspa f	dandruff
castaña f	chestnut
castañuelas fpl	castanets
castellano(a)	Spanish ; Castilian
castillo m	castle
catalán(lana)	Catalonian
catedral f	cathedral
causa f	cause
a causa de	because of
causar	to cause
cava m	Champagne-style wine
caza f	hunting ; game
cazuela f	casserole
cebolla f	onion
cebolleta f	spring onion
cecina f	cured meat ; dried meat
ceder: ceda el paso	give way
CE f	EC
CEE f	EEC
cementerio m	cemetery
cena f	dinner ; supper
cenar	to have dinner (evening meal)
centralita f	switchboard
Centroamérica f	Central America

centro *m*	centre
centro de la ciudad	city centre
centro comercial	shopping centre
centro docente	educational institution
cera *f*	wax
cerámica *f*	ceramics ; pottery
cerca (de)	near ; close to
cercanías *fpl*	outskirts ; proximity
el tren de cercanías	suburban train
cerdo *m*	pig ; pork
cereal *m*	cereal
cereza *f*	cherry
cerilla *f*	match
cerrado(a)	closed ; shut ; off *(tap)*
cerrado por reforma	closed for repairs
cerrar	to close
cerro *m*	hill
certificado *m*	certificate
certificado de seguros	insurance certificate
certificado(a)	registered
certificar	to register
cervecería *f*	pub
cerveza *f*	beer ; lager
cerveza de barril	draught beer
césped *m*	lawn
cesta *f*	shopping basket
cestería *f*	basketwork *(shop)*
chalé *m*	villa
chaleco salvavidas *m*	life jacket
champán *m*	champagne
champiñón *m*	mushroom
champú *m*	shampoo
chanquetes *mpl*	whitebait
charcutería *f*	shop selling cooked pork meat

cheque *m*	cheque
cheque de viaje	traveller's cheque
chicle *m*	chewing gum
chicle sin azúcar	sugarfree chewing gum
chico(a) *adj*	small
chile *m*	chilli
chilindrón (al)	cooked in spicy sauce
chinchón *m*	aniseed liqueur
chiringuito *m*	bar
chocolate *m*	chocolate ; hot chocolate
chocolate con leche	milk chocolate
chocolate puro	plain chocolate
chocolatería *f*	café serving hot chocolate
chófer *m*	chauffeur ; driver
chopitos *mpl*	small squid
chorizo *m*	type of salami ; hard pork sausage
chuleta *f*	cutlet
chuleta de cerdo	pork chop
chuletas de cordero	lamb chops
chuletas de ternera	veal cutlets
chuletón *m*	beef chop
churrasco *m*	barbecued steak
churrería *f*	fritter shop or stand
churro *m*	fritter
ciclista *m/f*	cyclist
ciego(a)	blind
cielo *m*	sky
cien	hundred
ciento uno(a)	a hundred and one
CIF	tax number *(for business)*
cifra *f*	number ; figure
cigala *f*	crayfish ; Norway lobster
cigalas plancha	grilled crayfish
cigarra *f*	cicada
cigarrillo *m*	cigarette

cigarro m	cigar ; cigarette
cima f	top ; peak
cine m	cinema
cinta f	tape
cinta adhesiva	adhesive tape
cinta limpiadora	cleaning tape
cinta virgen	blank tape
cintura f	waist
cinturón m	belt
circo m	circus
circulación f	traffic
circular	to drive ; to circulate
circule por la derecha	keep right (road sign)
ciruela f	plum
cirujano(a) m/f	surgeon
cita f	appointment
ciudad f	city ; town
clara f	egg white
clarete m	light red wine
claro(a)	light (colour) ; clear
clase f	class ; type
clase preferente	club class
clase turista	economy class
clasificada X	adults only (film)
clavel m	carnation
cliente m/f	customer ; client
climatizado(a)	air-conditioned
clínica f	clinic ; private hospital
clínica dental	dental surgery
club nocturno m	night club
cobrador m	conductor (bus)
cobrar	to charge ; to cash
cobro m	payment
cocer	to cook ; to boil

coche *m*	car
coche de alquiler	hired car
coche-cama *m*	sleeping car
coche-comedor *m*	dining car
cocido *m*	thick stew
cocido(a)	cooked ; boiled
cocina *f*	kitchen ; cooker ; cuisine
cocinar	to cook
coco *m*	coconut
cóctel *m*	cocktail
código *m*	code
código postal	post-code
codorniz *f*	quail
codornices asadas	roast quail
coger	to catch ; to get ; to pick up *(phone)*
col *f*	cabbage
coles de Bruselas	Brussels sprouts
cola *f*	glue ; queue
colador *m*	strainer
colchón *m*	mattress
colchón neumático	air bed
colegio *m*	school
colgar	to hang up *(phone)*
coliflor *f*	cauliflower
colonia *f*	eau-de-Cologne
color *m*	colour
comedor *m*	dining room
comenzar	to begin
comer	to eat
comercio *m*	trade ; business
comestibles *mpl*	groceries
comida *f*	food ; meal
se sirven comidas	meals served
comidas caseras	home cooking

comisaría f	police station
como adv	as ; like
como conj	since
¿cómo?	how? ; pardon?
¿cómo está?	how are you?
¿cómo se llama?	what is your name?
compañero m	colleague ; classmate
compañía f	company
compartimiento m	compartment
completo(a)	full up (bus, etc.) ; complete
completo	no vacancies (hotel, etc.)
comportarse	to behave
compra f	purchase
compras	shopping
comprar	to buy
comprender	to understand
compresas fpl	sanitary towels
comprobar	to check
compruebe su cambio	please check your change
con	with
coñac m	cognac ; brandy
concha f	sea-shell
concierto m	concert
concurrido(a)	busy
concurso m	competition
condición f	condition
condimento m	seasoning
conducir	to drive
conductor(a) m/f	driver
conectar	to connect ; to plug in
conejo m	rabbit
conejo guisado	rabbit stew
confitería f	confectioner's ; cake shop
confitura f	jam

congelado(a)	frozen
congelador m	freezer
congrio m	conger eel
congrio asado	baked conger eel
conjunto m	group (music)
conocer	to know ; to be acquainted with
conserje m	caretaker
conservar	to keep
conserve su billete	please keep your ticket
conservas fpl	tinned foods
consigna f	left-luggage office
consigna automática	left-luggage locker
consomé m	consommé
consomé de ave	chicken consommé
consomé de gallina	chicken consommé
consulado m	consulate
consultorio m	surgery ; doctor's office
consumición mínima	cover charge
consumir	to eat ; to use
consumir antes de...	best before...
contacto m	contact ; ignition (car)
contador m	meter
contenido m	contents
contento(a)	pleased
contestar	to answer
contrato m	contract
control m	inspection ; check
convento m	convent ; monastery
copa f	glass ; goblet
copa de helado	mixed ice cream
tomar una copa	to have a drink
corazón m	heart
corbata f	tie
cordero m	lamb ; mutton
cordero asado	roast lamb

cordillera f	mountain range
correo m	mail
Correos m	post office
corrida de toros f	bullfight
corriente f	power ; current *(electricity, etc.)*
corriente *adj*	ordinary ; normal
cortado m	small coffee with dash of milk
corte m	cut
corte de helado	ice-cream wafer
corte de pelo	haircut
cortina f	curtain
cosecha f	harvest; vintage *(wine)*
costa f	coast
costar	to cost
costero(a)	coastal
costilla f	rib
coto m	reserve
coto de caza	hunting by licence
coto de pesca	fishing by licence
crédito m	credit
a crédito	on credit
creer	to think ; to believe
crema f	cream
crema de afeitar	shaving cream
crema bronceadora	suntan lotion
cremallera f	zip
cristalería f	glassware *(shop)* ; glazier's
cruce m	junction ; crossroads
crucero m	cruise
cruzar	to cross
c/u (cada uno)	each (one)
cuaderno m	exercise book
cuadro m	picture ; painting
a cuadros	checked *(pattern)*
cuajada f	curd

cuando/¿cuándo?	when ; when?
¿cuánto(a)?	how much?
cuarentena f	quarantine
cuarto m	room ; quarter
cuarto de baño	bathroom
cubalibre m	rum and coke
cubertería f	cutlery
cubierta f	deck
cubierto(a)	covered ; indoor
cubiertos	cutlery
cubierto no. 3	menu no. 3
cubo m	bucket ; pail
cubo de la basura	dustbin
cubrir	to cover
cuchara f	spoon ; tablespoon
cuello m	collar ; neck
cuenta f	bill ; account *(at bank, shop)*
cuenta de ahorros	savings account
cuenta bancaria	bank account
cuenta corriente	current account
cuerda f	string ; rope
cuero m	leather
cuerpo m	body
cueva f	cave
cuidado m	care
¡cuidado!	look out!
ten cuidado	take care!
cuidar	to look after
cultivar	to grow ; to farm
cumpleaños m	birthday
¡feliz cumpleaños!	happy birthday!
cuna f	cradle ; cot
"curasán" m	croissant
curva f	bend ; curve
curvas peligrosas	dangerous bends

Spanish	English
Damas *fpl*	**Ladies**
daño *m*	**damage**
dar	**to give**
dátil *m*	**date** *(fruit)*
datos *mpl*	**data ; information**
datos personales	personal details
DCHA.	*abbrev. for* **derecha**
de	**of ; from**
debajo	**under ; underneath**
deber	**to owe**
debido(a)	**due**
declarar	**to declare**
dedo *m*	**finger**
dedo del pie	toe
defecto *m*	**fault ; defect**
degustación *f*	**sampling ; tasting** *(wine, etc.)*
dejar	**to let**
dejar libre la salida	keep exit clear
delante de	**in front of**
delegación *f*	**police station** *(Lat. Am.)*
delgado(a)	**thin ; slim**
delicado(a)	**delicate**
demora *f*	**delay**
denominación de	**guarantee of quality**
origen	of wine
dentífrico *m*	**toothpaste**
dentista *m/f*	**dentist**
dentro (de)	**inside**
departamento *m*	**compartment ; department**
dependienta *f*	**sales assistant**
dependiente *m/f*	**sales assistant**
deporte *m*	**sport**
deportivo(a)	**sporty**
depósito de gasolina *m*	**petrol tank**

derecha *f*	right(-hand side)
a la derecha	on/to the right
derecho *m*	right ; law
derechos de aduana	customs duty
derecho(a)	right ; straight
desabrochar	to unfasten
desayuno *m*	breakfast
descafeinado(a)	decaffeinated
descalzo(a)	barefoot
descansar	to rest
descanso *m*	rest ; half-time ; interval
descarga (electrica) *f*	shock *(electric)*
descargado(a)	flat *(battery)*
descolgar	to take down ; to pick up *(phone)*
descongelar	to defrost ; to thaw ; to de-ice
descuento *m*	discount
desde	since ; from
desear	to want
desembarcadero *m*	quay
desembarcar	to land ; to disembark
desenchufado(a)	off ; disconnected
deseo *m*	wish ; desire
desfile *m*	parade
deshacer	to undo ; to unpack
desinfectante *m*	disinfectant
desmaquillador *m*	make-up remover
desnatado(a)	skimmed
desnudarse	to get undressed
desodorante *m*	deodorant
despacho *m*	office
despacho de billetes	ticket office
despacio	slowly ; quietly
despegue *m*	takeoff *(of plane)*
despertador *m*	alarm *(clock)*

despertarse	to wake up
después	after ; afterward(s)
desteñir: no destiñe	colourfast
destino m	destination
desvestirse	to get undressed
desvío m	detour ; diversion
detalle m	detail ; nice gesture
al detalle	retail (commercial)
detergente m	detergent
detrás (de)	behind
devolver	to give back ; to put back
devuelve cambio	change given (vending machine, etc.)
día m	day
todo el día	all day
día festivo	public holiday
día laborable	working day
diabético(a) m/f	diabetic
diapositiva f	slide (photo)
diario m	newspaper
diario(a)	daily
diarrea f	diarrhoea
diente m	tooth
diez	ten
difícil	difficult
dinero	money
dirección f	direction ; address
dirección particular	home address
dirección prohibida	no entry
dirección única	one-way
directo(a)	direct
director(a) m/f	director ; manager
director gerente	managing director
dirigirse a	to go towards ; to speak to
disco m	record ; disk
discoteca f	disco

discrecional	**optional**
diseño m	**design ; drawing**
disfraz m	**mask ; fancy dress**
disminuir	**to lower** (temperature) **; to decrease**
disolver	**to dissolve**
disponible	**available**
distancia f	**distance**
divisa f	**foreign currency**
doblado(a)	**dubbed** (film)
doble	**double**
docena f	**dozen**
documentación f	**papers ; documents**
dólar m	**dollar**
dolor m	**ache ; pain**
dolor de cabeza	**headache**
dolor de garganta	**sore throat**
dolor de muelas	**toothache**
domicilio m	**home address**
domingo m	**Sunday**
donde/¿dónde?	**where/where?**
dorada f	**sea bream**
dormir	**to sleep**
dorso m	**back**
véase al dorso	**PTO (please turn over)**
dosis f	**dose ; dosage**
droguería f	**cleaning material shop**
ducha f	**shower**
dueño(a) m/f	**owner**
dulce adj	**sweet**
el agua dulce	**fresh water**
dulce m	**dessert**
durante	**during**
durazno m	**peach**
duro(a)	**hard**

echar	to pour ; to throw
edad f	age (of person)
edad mínima	age limit
edificio m	building
EE.UU.	abbrev. for Estados Unidos (USA)
efecto m	effect
efectos personales	belongings
ejemplar m	copy (of book)
el	the
él	he ; him
electricidad f	electricity
eléctrico(a)	electric(al)
elegir	to choose
elevador m	lift ; elevator
ella	she ; her
ellas	they
ello	it
ellos	they
embajada f	embassy
embalse m	reservoir
embarazo m	pregnancy
embarcadero m	jetty
embarcarse	to board
embarque m	boarding
embutidos mpl	various types of sausage
emergencia f	emergency
emisión f	broadcasting (radio, TV)
emitido por	issued by
empachado	upset (stomach)
empanada f	type of pasty/pie
empanadilla f	pasty with savoury filling
empanado(a)	fried in breadcrumbs
empaste m	filling (in tooth)
empezar	to begin

empleo *m*	employment ; use
empresa *f*	firm
empujar	to push
empujad	push *(on door)*
empuje	push *(on door)*
en	in ; into ; on
encaje *m*	lace
encargado(a) *m/f*	person in charge
encargar	to order in advance *(food, etc.)*
encendedor *m*	cigarette lighter
encender	to switch on ; to light
encender las luces	switch on headlights
encendido *m*	ignition
encendido(a)	on *(switch)*
enchilada *f*	rolled filled tortilla
enchufar	to plug in
enchufe *m*	plug ; point ; socket
encía *f*	gum
encima de	onto ; on top of
encogerse	to shrink
encontrar	to find
encurtidos *mpl*	pickles
endibias *fpl*	endives
enero *m*	January
enfermera *f*	nurse
enfermería *f*	infirmary ; first-aid post
enfermo(a)	ill
enfrente (de)	opposite
enjuagar	to rinse
enlace *m*	connection *(train, plane, etc.)*
enlazar	to connect
ensalada *f*	salad
ensalada de lechuga	green salad
ensalada mixta	mixed salad

enseñar	to show ; to teach
entender	to understand
entero(a)	whole
entrada f	entrance ; ticket ; admission
precio de entrada	admission fee
entrada libre	admission free
entrada por delante	entrance at the front
entrantes mpl	starters
entrar	to go in ; to come in
entre	among ; between
entreacto m	interval
entrecot m	rib steak
entregar	to deliver
entremeses mpl	hors d'oeuvres
envase m	container ; packaging
enviar	to send
envío m	shipment
envolver	to wrap
equipaje m	luggage ; baggage
equipaje de mano	hand-luggage
equipaje permitido	luggage allowance
equipo m	team ; equipment
equitación f	horseriding
equivocación f	mistake
es	he/she/it is
escabechado(a)	pickled
escabeche m	spicy marinade
escala f	stopover
escalera f	flight of steps ; stairs ; ladder
escalera de incendios	fire escape
escalera mecánica	escalator
escalón m	step (stair)
escalope m	escalope
escalope de ternera	veal escalope
escaparate m	shop window

escenario *m*	theatre stage
escoger	to choose
escribir	to write
escrito: por escrito	in writing
escuchar	to listen to
escuela *f*	school
escurrir	to wring
esmalte *m*	varnish
espacio *m*	space
espaguetis *mpl*	spaghetti
España *f*	Spain
español(a)	Spanish
esparadrapo *m*	sticking plaster
espárrago *m*	asparagus
especialidad *f*	speciality
espectáculo *m*	entertainment ; show
espejo *m*	mirror
espejo retrovisor	rear-view mirror
espera *f*	wait
esperar	to wait (for)
espere su turno	please wait your turn
espinaca *f*	spinach
esposa *f*	wife
esposo *m*	husband
espuma *f*	foam
espuma de afeitar	shaving foam
espumoso(a)	frothy ; sparkling
espumoso	sparkling wine
esq.	*abbrev. for* esquina
esquí *m*	skiing ; ski
esquí acuático	water-skiing
esquina *f*	street corner
está	you/he/she/it is
establecimiento *m*	shop ; establishment

estación *f*	railway station ; season
estación de servicio	petrol station
estacionamiento *m*	parking space
estacionar	to park
estadio *m*	stadium ; football ground
Estados Unidos *mpl*	United States
estanco *m*	tobacconist's
estar	to be *see* GRAMMAR
este *m*	east
estofado *m*	stew
estos(as)	these
estrecho(a)	narrow
estrella *f*	star
estreñimiento *m*	constipation
estreno *m*	première ; new release
estropeado(a)	out of order
estudiante *m/f*	student
etiqueta *f*	label ; ticket ; tag
de etiqueta	formal *(dress)*
evitar	to avoid
exceso *m*	excess
exceso de equipaje	excess baggage
excursión *f*	tour ; excursion ; outing
excursión a pie	hike
excusado *m*	toilet *(Lat. Am.)*
éxito *m*	success
expedido(a)	issued
explicar	to explain
exponer	to expose ; to explain
exposición *f*	exhibition
expreso *m*	express train
extintor *m*	fire extinguisher
extranjero(a) *m/f*	foreigner
en el extranjero	abroad

fabada f	pork and bean stew
fábrica f	factory
fácil	easy
factura f	receipt ; bill
facturación f	check-in
faisán m	pheasant
falda f	skirt
familia f	family
farmacia f	chemist's shop
farmacia de guardia	duty chemist
faro m	headlamp ; lighthouse
faro antiniebla	fog-lamp
favor m	favour
por favor	please
f.c.	*abbrev. for* **ferrocarril**
febrero m	February
fecha f	date
fecha de adquisición	date of purchase
fecha de caducidad	expiry date ; best before
fecha de expedición	date of issue
fecha de nacimiento	date of birth
feliz	happy
femenino(a)	feminine
feria f	trade fair ; funfair
ferretería f	ironmonger's
ferrocarril (f.c.) m	railway
festivos mpl	public holidays
fiambre m	cold meat
ficha f	token ; counter
fichero m	file *(computer)*
fideos mpl	noodles
fiebre f	fever
fiesta f	party ; public holiday
fila f	row

filete *m*	fillet
filial *f*	branch
fin *m*	end
fin de semana	weekend
finalizar	to end ; to finish
finca *f*	farm ; property
fino *m*	light, dry, very pale sherry
firma *f*	signature
firmar	to sign
firme aquí	sign here *(on forms)*
firme deslizante	slippery surface *(road)*
flan *m*	crème caramel
flete *m*	freight
flor *f*	flower
flúor *m*	fluoride
foco *m*	spotlight ; headlamp
foie-gras *m*	liver pâté
folleto *m*	leaflet
fonda *f*	inn ; tavern ; small restaurant
forfait *m*	lift pass *(skiing)*
formulario *m*	form
fósforo *m*	match
foto *f*	picture ; photo
fotocopia *f*	photocopy
fotógrafo(a) *m/f*	photographer
frágil	handle with care
frambuesa *f*	raspberry
francés(esa)	French
Francia *f*	France
frase *f*	phrase ; sentence
fregar los platos	to do the washing up
frenar	to brake
freno *m*	brake
frente *f*	forehead

frente a	opposite
fresa f	strawberry
fresco(a)	fresh ; crisp ; cool
fresón m	large strawberry
frigorífico m	refrigerator
fríjol m	kidney bean
frío(a)	cold ; chilled
frito(a)	fried
fritura f	fried dishes
frontera f	border ; frontier
frotar	to rub
fruta f	fruit
fruta del tiempo	fresh fruit of the season
frutería f	fruit shop
frutos secos m	dried fruit and nuts
fuego m	fire
fuegos artificiales	fireworks
fuente f	fountain
fuera	outdoors ; out
fuerte	strong ; loud
fuerza f	force ; strength
fumador(a) m/f	smoker
fumar	to smoke
prohibido fumar	no smoking
función f	show
funcionar	to work
no funciona	out of order
funcionario(a) m/f	civil servant
funda f	crown (for tooth) ; pillowcase
furgoneta f	van
fusible m	fuse

gafas *fpl*	glasses
gafas de sol	sunglasses
galería de arte *f*	art gallery
gallego(a)	Galician
galleta *f*	biscuit
gamba *f*	prawn
gambas al ajillo	garlic-fried prawns
gambas al pil-pil	spicy prawns
gambas a la plancha	grilled prawns
ganar	to earn ; to win *(sports, games, etc.)*
garaje *m*	garage
garantía *f*	guarantee
garbanzo *m*	chickpea
garganta *f*	throat
gas *m*	gas
gas butano	Calor gas®
con gas	fizzy
sin gas	non-fizzy
gasa *f*	gauze ; nappy
gaseosa *f*	lemonade ; fizzy drink
gasoil *m*	diesel fuel
gasóleo *m*	diesel oil
gasolina *f*	petrol
gasolina sin plomo	unleaded petrol
gasolina super	4-star petrol
gasolinera *f*	petrol station
gato *m*	jack *(for car)*
gazpacho *m*	cold tomato and vegetable soup
gendarme *m/f*	policeman/woman *(Lat. Am.)*
gendarmería *f*	police *(Lat. Am.)*
género *m*	type ; material
gerente *m/f*	manager/manageress
ginebra *f*	gin
giro postal *m*	money order ; postal order

glorieta *f*	roundabout
goma *f*	rubber
gorro de baño *m*	bathing cap
gracias	thank you
grada *f*	tier
granada *f*	pomegranate
gran (+ noun)	great
Gran Bretaña *f*	Great Britain
grande	large ; big ; tall
grandes almacenes *mpl*	department stores
granja *f*	farm
gratinado(a)	au gratin
grifo *m*	tap
gripe *f*	flu
grúa *f*	crane ; breakdown van
grupo *m*	party ; group
grupo sanguíneo	blood group
guacamole *m*	avocado dip *(Lat. Am.)*
guardacostas *m*	coastguard
guardar	to put away ; to keep
guardarropa *m*	cloakroom
guardería *f*	nursery
guardia *f*	guard
Guardia Civil	Civil Guard
Guardia Nacional	National Guard
de guardia	on duty
guarnición *f*	garnish
guía *m/f*	courier ; guide
Guía del ocio	What's on *(magazine)*
guía telefónica	telephone directory
guindilla *f*	chilli pepper
guisantes *mpl*	peas
guiso *m*	stew
gustar	to like ; to enjoy

haba *f*	broad bean
habano *m*	Havana cigar
habichuelas *fpl*	haricot beans
habitación *f*	room
habitación doble	double room
habitación individual	single room
hablar	to speak
se habla inglés	English spoken
hacer	to do ; to make
hacia	toward(s)
hacia adelante	forwards
hacia atrás	backwards
hacienda *f*	farm ; ranch *(Lat. Am.)*
hamburguesa *f*	hamburger
hasta	until ; till
hay	there is/there are
hecho(a)	finished ; done
hecho a mano	handmade
hecho a la medida	made to measure
helada *f*	frost
peligro – heladas	danger – ice on road
heladería *f*	ice-cream parlour
helado *m*	ice cream
helado de mantecado	vanilla ice cream
helado de nata	plain ice cream
helado de turrón	almond ice cream
hemorragia *f*	haemorrhage
hemorroides *fpl*	haemorrhoids
herida *f*	wound
hermana *f*	sister
hermano *m*	brother
herramienta *f*	tool
hervir	to boil
hielo *m*	ice
con hielo	with ice

hierbabuena f	mint
hlerro m	iron (metal)
hígado m	liver
hígado con cebollı	fried liver with onions
higo m	fig
higos chumbos	prickly pears
hija f	daughter
hijo m	son
hilo m	thread
hipermercado m	hypermarket
hípica f	showjumping
hipódromo m	racecourse
hogar m	home ; household
hoja f	leaf ; sheet (of paper)
hojaldre m	puff pastry
hola	hello
hombre m	man
hora f	hour
horario m	timetable
horchata de chufa f	refreshing tigernut drink
hormiga f	ant
horno m	oven
al horno	baked ; roasted
hostal m	small hotel
hoy	today
huachinango m	red snapper (Lat. Am.)
hueso m	bone
huésped(a) m/f	host ; guest
huevo m	egg
huevos de aldea	free-range eggs
huevos duros	hard-boiled eggs
huevos escalfados	poached eggs
huevos al plato	baked eggs
huevos revueltos	scrambled eggs
humo m	smoke

ida *f*	outward journey
de ida y vuelta	return *(ticket)*
idioma *m*	language
iglesia *f*	church
igual	equal
impar	odd *(number)*
impermeable *m*	raincoat
importe *m*	amount
impreso *m*	form
impresos *mpl*	printed matter
incendio *m*	fire
incluido(a)	included
inclusive	including
indicaciones *fpl*	directions
índice *m*	index
individual	individual ; single
infección *f*	infection
inferior	inferior ; lower
inflamación *f*	inflammation
información *f*	information (office)
infracción *f*	offence
infracción de tráfico	traffic offence
Inglaterra *f*	England ; Britain
inglés(esa)	English ; British
inoxidable	stainless ; rustproof
inquilino(a) *m/f*	tenant
insolación *f*	sunstroke
instituto *m*	institute ; secondary school
instituto de belleza	beauty salon
instrucciones *fpl*	directions ; instructions
integral: pan integral	wholemeal bread
interés *m*	interest
interior	inside
internacional	international

intérprete *m/f*	**interpreter**
interruptor *m*	**switch**
introducir	**to introduce ; to insert**
introduzca monedas	**insert coins**
invierno *m*	**winter**
invitación *f*	**invitation**
invitado(a) *m/f*	**guest**
inyección *f*	**injection**
ir	**to go**
isla *f*	**island**
itinerario *m*	**route**
IVA	**VAT**
izquierda *f*	**left**
izquierdo(a)	**left**
IZQ. / IZQDA.	*abbrev. for* **izquierda**

jabón *m*	**soap**
jabón en polvo	**soap powder**
jamás	**never**
jamón *m*	**ham**
jamón de Jabugo	**Andalucian cured ham**
jamón serrano	**cured ham**
jamón York	**boiled ham**
jaqueca *f*	**migraine**
jarabe *m*	**syrup**
jarabe para la tos	**cough syrup**
jardín *m*	**garden**
jardín botánico	**botanical gardens**
jarra *f*	**jug ; mug**
jefe(a) *m/f*	**chief ; head ; boss**
jerez *m*	**sherry**
joya *f*	**jewel**
joyas	**jewellery**
joyas de fantasía	**imitation jewellery**

joyería f	jeweller's
jubilado(a) m/f	pensioner ; senior citizen
judías fpl	beans
judías blancas	white haricot beans
judías verdes	French beans
juego m	game
juez(a) m/f	judge
jugador(a) m/f	player
jugar	to play ; to gamble
jugo m	juice
juguetería f	toy shop
junto(a)	together
junto a	next to
juvenil	youthful
juventud f	youth
kilo m	kilo
kilometraje m	= *mileage*
kilometraje ilimitado	unlimited mileage
kilómetro m	kilometre
la	the ; her ; it
labio m	lip
laborable	working *(day)*
laborables	weekdays
laca f	hair spray
lado m	side
al lado de	beside
lago m	lake
lana f	wool
lancha f	launch
lancha motora	motorboat

langosta *f*	lobster
langostino *m*	king prawn
largo(a)	long
largo recorrido	long-distance *(train, etc.)*
las	them ; the
lata *f*	can *(container)* ; tin
lateral	side
lavable	washable
lavabo *m*	lavatory ; washbasin
lavadero *m*	laundry room
lavado(a)	washed
lavado en seco	dry-cleaning
lavado y marcado	shampoo and set
lavadora *f*	washing machine
lavandería *f*	laundry
lavar	to wash
lavarse	to wash oneself
laxante *m*	laxative
leche *f*	milk
leche condensada	condensed milk
leche de vaca	cow's milk
leche desnatada	skimmed milk
leche entera	full cream milk
leche merengada	milk and egg sorbet
lechón *m*	sucking pig
lechuga *f*	lettuce
leer	to read
legumbres *fpl*	pulses
lejía *f*	bleach
lencería *f*	lingerie ; linen ; draper's
lengua *f*	language ; tongue
lenguas de gato	sponge fingers
lenguado *m*	sole ; lemon sole
lente *f*	lens
lentes de contacto	contact lenses

lentejas *fpl*	**lentils**
lentillas *fpl*	**contact lenses**
levantar	**to lift**
levantarse	**to get up ; to rise**
libra *f*	**pound** (currency, weight)
libra esterlina	**pound sterling** (£)
libre	**free ; vacant ; for hire** (taxi)
libre de impuestos	**tax-free**
dejen el paso libre	**keep clear**
librería *f*	**bookshop**
libro *m*	**book**
licencia *f*	**permit ; licence**
licenciarse	**to graduate**
licor *m*	**liqueur**
licores *mpl*	**spirits**
lidia *f*	**bullfight**
liebre *f*	**hare**
lima *f*	**file** (for nails) ; **lime**
límIte *m*	**limit ; boundary**
límite de velocidad	**speed limit**
limón *m*	**lemon**
limonada *f*	**lemonade**
limpiar	**to clean**
limpieza en seco *f*	**dry-cleaning**
lindo(a)	**nice** (Lat. Am.)
línea *f*	**line**
líneas aéreas	**airlines**
lino *m*	**linen**
linterna *f*	**torch**
liquidación *f*	**sales**
líquido *m*	**liquid**
liso(a)	**plain ; smooth**
lista *f*	**list**
lista de correos	**poste restante**
lista de precios	**price list**

listo(a)	ready ; clever
llsto(a) para comer	ready-cooked
litera f	bunk ; berth ; couchette
litoral m	coast
litro m	litre
llamada f	call
llamada telefónica	telephone call
llamada urbana	local call
llamar	to call ; to phone
llanta f	tyre
llave f	key ; tap ; spanner
Lleg.	*abbrev. for* llegada
llegada f	arrival
llegadas (Lleg.)	arrivals
llegar	to arrive ; to come
llenar	to fill ; to fill in
lleno(a)	full (up)
llevar	to bring ; to wear ; to carry
para llevar	to take away
lluvia f	rain
local m	premises ; bar
localidad f	place
localidades fpl	tickets (theatre)
loción f	lotion
loncha f	slice (ham, etc.)
Londres m	London
lubina f	bass
luces fpl	lights
lugar m	place
lugar de nacimiento	place of birth
lugar de expedición	issued in
lugar fresco	cool place
lujo m	luxury
luna f	moon
luz f	light

macedonia de frutas *f*	**fruit salad**
maceta *f*	**flowerpot**
madera *f*	**wood**
madre *f*	**mother**
maíz *m*	**maize**
malo(a)	**bad**
maleta *f*	**case ; suitcase**
Mallorca *f*	**Majorca**
malo(a)	**bad**
mañana	**tomorrow**
la mañana	**morning**
mancha *f*	**stain**
mandarina *f*	**tangerine**
manera *f*	**way ; manner**
manga *f*	**sleeve**
mano *f*	**hand**
de segunda mano	**used ; secondhand**
manta *f*	**blanket**
mantel *m*	**tablecloth**
mantener	**to maintain ; to keep**
mantequería *f*	**dairy** *(shop)*
mantequilla *f*	**butter**
manzana *f*	**apple ; block** *(of houses)*
manzanilla *f*	**camomile tea ; dry sherry**
mapa *m*	**map**
mapa de carreteras	**road map**
maquillaje *m*	**make-up**
máquina *f*	**machine**
máquina de afeitar	**razor**
máquina de fotos	**camera**
mar *m*	**sea**
marcar	**to dial ; to score**
marea *f*	**tide**
marea alta/baja	**high/low tide**

mareo m	seasickness ; giddiness
marfil m	ivory
margarina f	margarine
marido m	husband
marinera (a la)	in fish or seafood sauce
mariscos mpl	seafood ; shellfish
marisquería f	seafood restaurant
marroquí	Moroccan
marroquinería f	leather goods
más	more ; plus
material m	material
matrícula f	registration number ; number plate
matrimonio m	marriage
máximo m	maximum
mayo m	May
mayonesa f	mayonnaise
mayores de 18 años	over-18s
mayúscula f	capital letter
mazapán m	marzipan
mecánico m	mechanic
mechero m	lighter
medallones mpl	medallions (meat)
mediano(a)	medium ; middling
medianoche f	midnight
medianoches	small slightly sweet buns
mediante	by means of
medias fpl	tights
medicamentos mpl	medicines
medicina f	medicine ; drug
médico(a) m/f	doctor
medida f	measurement ; size
medio(a)	half
medio m	the middle
media hora	half an hour

mediodía m	midday ; noon
mejicano(a) m/f	Mexican
Méjico m	Mexico
mejilla f	cheek
mejillón m	mussel
melaza f	molasses ; treacle
melocotón m	peach
melón m	melon
melón con jamón	melon with cured ham
membrillo m	quince
menaje m	kitchen utensils
menaje de hogar	household goods
menestra f	vegetable stew
menor	smaller/smallest ; least
Menorca f	Minorca
menos	minus ; less ; except
mensaje m	message
mensual	monthly
menta f	mint ; peppermint
mentolado(a)	mentholated
menú m	menu
menú fijo	set menu ; table d'hôte
menú del día	menu of the day
menudillos mpl	giblets
mercado m	market
Mercado Común m	Common Market
mercancías fpl	goods
mercería f	haberdasher's
merendero m	open-air snack bar
merengue m	meringue
merienda f	afternoon snack ; picnic
merluza f	hake
merluza a la plancha	grilled hake
merluza a la romana	hake fried in batter

mermelada f	jam ; marmalade
mes m	month
mesa f	table
mesón m	traditional type restaurant
metro m	metre ; underground
mezcla f	mixture
mezquita f	mosque
miel f	honey
mientras	while
migas fpl	fried breadcrumbs
migraña f	migraine
mil	thousand
milagro m	miracle
mimbre m	wicker
mínimo m	minimum
ministerio m	ministry
minusválido(a)	handicapped ; disabled
minuto m	minute
misa f	mass
mismo(a)	same
mitad f	half
mixto(a)	mixed
moda f	fashion
modelo m	model
modo m	way ; manner
modo de empleo	instructions for use
mole m	black chilli sauce *(Lat. Am.)*
molestar: no molestar	do not disturb
molestia f	bother ; nuisance ; discomfort
molido(a)	ground *(coffee beans, etc.)*
molino m	mill
molino de viento	windmill
mollejas fpl	sweetbreads
monasterio m	monastery

moneda f	currency ; coin
introduzca monedas	insert coins
moneda extranjera	foreign currency
montaña f	mountain
montañismo m	mountaineering
montar	to ride
montar a caballo	to ride a horse
montilla m	a sherry-type wine
mora f	mulberry ; blackberry
morcilla f	black pudding
mosca f	fly
mostaza f	mustard
mosto m	grape juice
mostrador m	counter
mostrar	to show
motocicleta f	motorbike
motor m	engine ; motor
mover	to move
muchedumbre f	crowd
mucho(a)	a lot (of) ; much
mucho adv	a lot
muebles mpl	furniture (shop)
muela f	tooth
muelle m	quay ; pier
muerto(a)	dead
muestra f	exhibition ; sample
mujer f	woman ; wife
multa f	fine
muñeca f	wrist ; doll
muro m	wall
museo m	museum
música f	music
muslo m	thigh
muy	very

nabo *m*	turnip
nácar *m*	mother-of-pearl
nacimiento *m*	birth
nación *f*	nation
nacional	national
nacionalidad *f*	nationality
nada	nothing
de nada	don't mention it
nadador(a) *m/f*	swimmer
nadar	to swim
naipes *mpl*	playing cards
naranja *f*	orange
naranjada *f*	orangeade
nariz *f*	nose
nata *f*	cream
nata batida	whipped cream
natación *f*	swimming
natillas *fpl*	egg custard
natural	natural ; fresh
naturaleza *f*	nature
naturista	naturist
navaja *f*	pocketknife ; penknife
Navidad *f*	Christmas
neblina *f*	mist
necesario(a)	necessary
necesitar	to need
negocios *mpl*	business
negro(a)	black
neumático *m*	tyre
nevera *f*	refrigerator
NIF	tax number *(of company)*
niebla *f*	fog
nieve *f*	snow
niña *f*	girl ; baby girl

ningún/ninguno(a)	none
niño m	boy ; baby; child
níspero m	medlar
nivel m	level ; standard
N°	*abbrev. for* número
noche f	night
esta noche	tonight
nochebuena f	Christmas Eve
nochevieja f	New Year's Eve
nocivo(a)	harmful
nombre m	name
nombre de pila	first name
norte m	north
Norteamérica f	America ; USA
nota f	note ; mark *(school)*
notaría f	solicitor's office
notario(a) m/f	notary ; solicitor
noticias fpl	news
novia f	girlfriend ; fiancée
noviembre m	November
novio m	boyfriend ; fiancé
nube f	cloud
nublado(a)	cloudy
nudillo m	knuckle
nudo(a)	nude
nuestro(a)	our
nuevo(a)	new
nuez f	nut ; walnut
nuez moscada	nutmeg
número m	number ; size ; issue
nunca	never

o	or
o ... o ...	either ... or ...
objetivo *m*	lens *(photography)*
objeto *m*	object
objetos de valor	valuables
objetos de regalo	gifts
obras *fpl*	road works
observar	to watch
obstruir	to block
océano *m*	ocean
ocio *m*	spare time
ocupado(a)	engaged ; busy
oeste *m*	west
oferta *f*	special offer
oficina *f*	office
Oficina de Correos *f*	Post Office
oficio *m*	church service ; profession
ofrecer	to offer
oído *m*	ear
ojo *m*	eye
¡ojo!	look out!
olla *f*	pot
olla de garbanzos	chick-pea stew
olor *m*	smell
oloroso *m*	cream sherry
olvidar	to forget
onda *f*	wave
operador(a) *m/f*	telephone operator
oporto *m*	port wine
oportunidades *fpl*	bargains
óptica *f*	optician's
orden *f*	command
ordenador *m*	computer
orilla *f*	shore

oro *m*	gold
orquesta *f*	orchestra
oscuro(a)	dark ; dim
ostra *f*	oyster
otoño *m*	autumn
otro(a)	other
oveja *f*	sheep
oxidado(a)	rusty

padre *m*	father
padres	parents
paella *f*	paella *(rice, saffron, seafood/chicken)*
pagado(a)	paid
pagar	to pay for ; to pay
pagar al contado	to pay cash
pagaré *m*	IOU
pago *m*	payment
pago por adelantado	payment in advance
pague en caja	please pay at cashdesk *(sign)*
país *m*	country
paisaje *m*	landscape ; countryside
pájaro *m*	bird
palacio *m*	palace
palabra *f*	word
palco *m*	box *(in theatre)*
palmera *f*	palm tree
palo *m*	stick ; mast
palo de golf	golf club
paloma *f*	pigeon
pan *m*	bread ; loaf of bread
pan de centeno	rye bread
pan integral	wholemeal bread
pan de molde	sliced bread
pan tostado	toast

panadería f	bakery
pañal m	nappy
panecillo m	bread roll
paño m	flannel ; cloth
pantalla f	screen
pantalones mpl	pair of trousers ; trousers
pantalones cortos	shorts
pantys mpl	tights
pañuelo m	handkerchief
pañuelo de papel	tissue (paper handkerchief)
papa f	potato (Lat. Am.)
papel m	paper
papel higiénico	toilet paper
papelería f	stationer's
papilla f	baby cereal
paquete m	packet ; parcel
par m	pair
par	even (number)
para	for; towards
parada f	stop
parada de autobús	bus stop
parada de taxis	taxi rank
parador m	state-run hotel
parar	to stop
¡pare!	stop!
pared f	wall
parque m	park
parque de atracciones	amusement park
parque de bomberos	fire station
parque zoológico	zoo
parrilla f	grill
a la parrilla	grilled
parrillada f	grilled meat or fish ; barbecue
parroquia f	parish church

particular	private
partida *f*	departure
partido *m*	match *(sport)*
partir	to depart
pasa *f*	raisin ; currant
pasaje *m*	alleyway
pasaje *m*	ticket ; fare
pasajero(a) *m/f*	passenger
pasaporte *m*	passport
pasatiempo *m*	hobby ; pastime
Pascua *f*	Easter
Pascua de Navidad	Christmas
¡felices Pascuas!	happy Christmas
pase sin llamar	enter without knocking *(sign)*
paseo *m*	walk ; avenue ; promenade
Paseo Colón	Columbus Avenue
paso *m*	step ; pace
paso de ganado	cattle crossing
paso inferior	subway
paso a nivel	level crossing
paso de peatones	pedestrian crossing
paso sin guarda	open level crossing
paso subterráneo	subway
pasos de contador	telephone meter units
pasta *f*	pastry ; pasta
pasta de dientes	toothpaste
pastel *m*	cake
pasteles	pastries
pastelería *f*	cakes and pastries
pastilla *f*	tablet *(medicine)*
pastilla de jabón	bar of soap
patata *f*	potato
patatas fritas	French fries ; crisps
patinaje *m*	skating
patinaje sobre hielo	ice-skating
pato *m*	duck

pavo *m*	turkey
pavo trufado	turkey with truffle stuffing
peaje *m*	toll
peatón *m*	pedestrian
peces *mpl*	fish
pechuga *f*	breast *(poultry)*
pedir	to ask for ; to order
pegamento *m*	gum ; glue
pegar	to stick (on)
p. ej.	*abbrev. for* por ejemplo
peladilla *f*	sugared almond
película *f*	film
peligro *m*	danger
peligro de incendio	danger of fire
peligroso(a)	dangerous
pelo *m*	hair
pelota *f*	ball ; Basque ball game
peluquería *f*	hairdresser's ; barber's
penicilina *f*	penicillin
pensión *f*	guesthouse
pensión completa	full board
media pensión	half board
peor	worse ; worst
pepinillo *m*	gherkin
pepino *m*	cucumber
pepitoria (en)	fricassée
pequeño(a)	little ; small
pera *f*	pear
perder	to lose ; to miss *(train, etc.)*
perdiz *f*	partridge
perdón *m*	pardon ; sorry
perdonar	to forgive
perejil *m*	parsley
perforar: no perforar	do not pierce

perfumería f	perfume shop
periódico m	newspaper
período m	period
perla f	pearl
permanente f	perm
permiso m	permission ; pass ; permit
permiso de conducir	driving licence
permiso de residencia	residence permit
permiso de trabajo	work permit
permitido(a)	permitted ; allowed
perro m	dog
perro caliente	hot dog
personal m	staff
pesado(a)	heavy ; boring ; rich (food)
pesca f	fishing
pescadería f	fishmonger's
pescadilla f	whiting ; baby hake
pescado m	fish
peso m	weight
pestiños mpl	crisp honey-fritters
pez m	fish
pez espada	swordfish
picadillo m	minced beef
picado(a)	chopped ; minced
picadura f	bite (insect) ; sting
picante	peppery ; hot ; spicy
picatostes mpl	fried bread
pie m	foot
piel f	fur ; skin ; leather
piel de carnero	sheepskin
pierna f	leg
pieza f	room ; part
pijama m	pyjamas
pila f	battery (radio, etc.)

píldora f	pill
pileta f	sink
pileta (de natación)	swimming pool *(Lat. Am.)*
pimentón m	paprika
pimienta f	pepper
a la pimienta	au poivre
pimiento m	pepper *(vegetable)*
pimiento verde/rojo	green/red pepper
pimiento morrón	red pepper
pimientos rellenos	stuffed peppers
piña f	pineapple
piña en almíbar	tinned pineapple
piña natural	fresh pineapple
pinacoteca f	art gallery
pinchar	to get a puncture/flat tyre
pinchos mpl	savoury titbits
pinchos morunos	kebabs
piñones mpl	pine kernels
pintura f	paint ; painting
pipirrana f	tomato and cucumber salad
piragua f	canoe
Pirineos mpl	Pyrenees
pisar	to step on ; to tread on
no pisar el césped	keep off the grass
piscina f	swimming pool
piso m	floor ; flat
piso deslizante	slippery road
pista f	track
pista de esquí	ski run
pista de patinaje	skating rink
pista de tenis	tennis court
pisto m	sautéed vegetables
placa f	licence plate
plancha f	iron *(for clothes)*
a la plancha	grilled
plano m	plan ; town map

planta f	plant ; sole (of foot)
planta baja	ground floor
plástico m	plastic
plata f	silver ; money
plata de ley	sterling silver
plátano m	banana
platea f	stalls (theatre)
platería f	jeweller's
plato m	plate ; dish (food) ; course
plato del día	set menu ; dish of the day
playa f	beach
playa nudista	nudist beach
plaza f	square
plaza del mercado	marketplace
plaza de toros	bull ring
plazas libres	vacancies ; parking spaces
plazas limitadas	limited number of seats
plazo m	period ; expiry date
poco(a)	little
un poco de	a bit of
pocos(as)	(a) few
podólogo(a) m/f	chiropodist
policía f	police
policía m/f	policeman/woman
Policía Municipal	traffic warden
póliza f	policy ; certificate
póliza de seguros	insurance policy
pollería f	poultry shop
pollo m	chicken
pollo al ajillo	garlic-fried chicken
pollo asado	roast chicken
pollo estofado	chicken casserole
poltrona f	armchair
polvo m	powder ; dust
polvos de talco	talcum powder
pomada f	ointment

pomelo *m*	grapefruit
ponche *m*	punch
poner	to put
por	for ; per ; through ; about
porcelana *f*	china ; porcelain
por favor	please
porrón *m*	glass wine jar with long spout
porrusalda *f*	cod potato and leek soup
portaequipajes *m*	luggage rack ; boot
portería *f*	caretaker's office
portero *m*	caretaker ; doorman
posología *f*	dosage
postal *f*	postcard
posterior	back
postre *m*	dessert ; sweet
potable	drinkable
potaje *m*	stew ; thick vegetable soup
potaje de garbanzos	thick chickpea soup
potaje de lentejas	thick lentil soup
pote *m*	stew
precio *m*	price
precipicio *m*	cliff
preciso(a)	precise ; necessary
preferir	to prefer
prefijo *m*	dialling code
preguntar	to ask
prensa *f*	press ; newspaper stand
presa *f*	dam
presentar	to introduce
presentarse	to check in
preservativo *m*	condom
presión *f*	pressure
primavera *f*	spring
primer/o(a)	first

principiante *m/f*	beginner
prioridad (de paso) *f*	right of way
prismáticos *mpl*	binoculars
privado(a)	personal ; private
probadores *mpl*	fitting rooms
probar	to try ; to sample ; to taste
procedencia *f*	point of departure
procedente de	coming from
productos *mpl*	produce ; products
profesión *f*	profession ; job
prohibido(a)	prohibited
prohibido bañarse	no bathing
prohibido el paso	no entry
pronóstico *m*	forecast
pronto	soon
propiedad *f*	property
propietario(a) *m/f*	owner
propina *f*	tip
propio(a)	own
provisional	temporary
próximo(a)	next
público(a)	public
puchero *m*	cooking pot ; stew
pueblo *m*	village ; country
puente *m*	bridge
puerro *m*	leek
puerta *f*	door ; gate
cierren la puerta	close the door
puerta de embarque	boarding gate
puerto *m*	port ; harbour ; pass *(mountain)*
pulpo *m*	octopus
puré *m*	purée
puré de patatas	mashed potatoes
puro(a)	pure

que	than
¿qué?	what? ; which?
¿qué tal?	how are you?
quedar	to remain ; to be left
queja f	complaint
quemadura f	burn
quemadura del sol	sunburn
queroseno m	paraffin
quesadilla f	light pastry/pie
queso m	cheese
queso de bola	round, mild cheese like Edam
queso de Burgos	fresh cheese
queso de cabra	goat's milk cheese
queso de Cabrales	very strong blue cheese
queso manchego	hard sheep's milk cheese
queso de nata	cream cheese
queso de oveja	sheep's milk cheese
quien/¿quién?	who ; who?
quisquilla f	shrimp
quita-esmalte m	nail polish remover
quitamanchas m	stain remover
quitar	to remove

rábano m	radish
rabo de buey m	oxtail
ración f	portion
raciones	snacks
radio f	radio ; radius
radiografía f	X-ray
ragout m	meat and vegetable stew
rápido m	express train ; heel bar
rápido(a)	quick ; fast
raqueta f	racket
Rastro m	flea market

ratero *m*	pickpocket
rato *m*	a while
razón *f*	reason
rebajas *fpl*	sale
rebozado(a)	cooked in batter
recambio *m*	spare ; refill
recepción *f*	reception ; reception desk
receta *f*	prescription ; recipe
recibo *m*	receipt
reclamación *f*	claim ; complaint
reclamar	to claim
recogida *f*	collection
recorrido *m*	journey ; route
de largo recorrido	long-distance
recuerdo *m*	souvenir
regadera *f*	shower
red *f*	net
reducción *f*	reduction
reembolso *m*	refund
refresco *m*	refreshment ; cold drink
refugio *m*	shelter
regalo *m*	gift ; present
régimen *m*	diet
región *f*	district ; area ; region
regla *f*	rule
rehogado(a)	fried in oil, garlic and vinegar
Reino Unido *m*	United Kingdom
reintegro *m*	**withdrawal** *(from bank account)*
rellenar	to fill in
relleno(a)	stuffed
remitente *m/f*	sender
remolacha *f*	beetroot
remolque *m*	tow rope ; trailer ; caravan

RENFE	**Spanish National Railways**
reparación f	**repair**
repollo m	**cabbage**
requesón m	**cheese similar to cottage cheese**
resbaladizo(a)	**slippery**
reserva f	**booking(s)**
reservar	**to reserve**
responder	**to answer ; to reply**
responsabilidad f	**responsibility**
restaurante m	**restaurant**
resto m	**the rest**
retraso m	**delay**
sin retraso	**on schedule**
revelado m	**developing** (of films)
revisar	**to check**
revisión t	**service** (for car) ; **inspection**
revista f	**magazine**
rincón m	**corner**
riñón m	**kidney**
río m	**river**
robo m	**robbery**
rodaballo m	**turbot**
rojo(a)	**red**
romana: a la romana	**fried in batter or breadcrumbs**
románico(a)	**Romanesque**
romería f	**pilgrimage**
romper	**to break ; to tear**
ron m	**rum**
ropa f	**clothes**
ropa interior	**underwear**
rosado m	**rosé**
rosbif m	**roast beef**
rueda f	**wheel**
ruido m	**noise**

SA	*abbrev. for* **Sociedad Anónima**
sábado *m*	Saturday
sábana *f*	sheet
saber	to know
sabor *m*	taste ; flavour
sacar	to take out
sacarina *f*	saccharin
saco *m*	sack
saco de dormir	sleeping bag
sagrado(a)	holy
sal *f*	salt
sin sal	unsalted
sala *f*	hall ; ward
sala de embarque	departure lounge
sala de espera	airport lounge ; waiting room
salado(a)	savoury ; salty
salario *m*	wage
salchicha *f*	sausage
salchichón *m*	salami sausage
saldo *m*	balance of account
saldos *mpl*	sales
salida *f*	exit ; departure ; socket
salir	to go out ; to come out
salmón *m*	salmon
salmonete *m*	red mullet
salón *m*	lounge *(in hotel)*
salón de juegos	amusement arcade
salsa *f*	gravy ; sauce ; dressing
salsa de tomate	tomato sauce
salsa verde	parsley garlic and onion sauce
salteado(a)	sauté, sautéed
salud *f*	health
¡salud!	cheers!
salvavidas *m*	lifebelt
sandía *f*	watermelon

sangrar	to bleed
sangría f	iced red wine and fruit punch
sardina f	sardine
sardina arenque	pilchard
sarpullido m	rash (on skin)
secado a mano m	blow-dry
secador de pelo m	hairdryer
secar	to dry
seco(a)	dry ; dried (fruit, beans)
seda f	silk
seguida: en seguida	straight away
seguido(a)	continuous
todo seguido	straight on
seguir	to continue ; to follow
según	according to
segundo(a)	second
de segunda mano	secondhand
seguramente	probably
seguridad f	security ; reliability; safety
seguro m	insurance
seguro(a)	safe ; for sure
sello m	stamp
semáforo m	traffic lights
semana f	week
Semana Santa	Holy Week ; Easter
semanal	weekly
señal f	sign ; signal
sencillo(a)	simple ; single (ticket)
señor m	gentleman
Señor (Sr.)	Mr. ; sir
señora f	lady
Señora (Sra.)	Mrs. ; Ms ; Madam
señorita f	Miss
Señorita (Srta.)...	Miss...

septentrional	northern
ser	to be *see* GRAMMAR
servicio *m*	service ; service charge
servicio incluido	service included
área de servicios	service area
servicios de urgencia	emergency services
servicios *mpl*	public conveniences
servir	to serve
sesión *f*	performance ; screening *(film)*
sesión de noche	late night performance
sesión numerada	seats bookable in advance
sesión de tarde	evening performance
sesos *mpl*	brains
seta *f*	mushroom
si	whether ; if
sí	yes
SIDA *m*	AIDS
sidra *f*	cider
siempre	always
siento: lo siento	I'm sorry
sierra *f*	mountain range
siga	follow
siga adelante	carry on
siga derecho	keep straight ahead
siguiente	following ; next
silencio *m*	silence
silla *f*	chair
silla de ruedas	wheelchair
simpático(a)	nice ; kind
sin	without
sinagoga *f*	synagogue
síntoma *m*	symptom
sírvase Vd. mismo	please serve yourself
sistema *m*	system
sitio *m*	place ; space ; position

Spanish	English
slip *m*	pants ; briefs
sobre	on ; upon
sobre *m*	envelope
sobrecarga *f*	surcharge
sociedad *f*	society
Sociedad Anónima	Ltd. ; plc
socio *m*	member ; partner
¡socorro!	help!
soja *f*	soya
sol *m*	sun ; sunshine
solamente	only
sólo	only
solo(a)	lone ; lonely
solomillo *m*	sirloin
solomillo a la broche	spit-roasted sirloin
soltero(a)	single
sombra *f*	shade ; shadow
sombrilla *f*	sunshade ; parasol
somnífero *m*	sleeping pill
sopa *f*	soup
sopa de ajo	garlic soup
sopa de cebolla	onion soup
sopa de pescado	fish soup
sopa sevillana	cream fish soup
sopa de verduras	vegetable soup
sorbete *m*	water ice
sordo(a)	deaf
sótano *m*	basement
soya *f*	soya
Sr.	*abbrev. for* **señor**
Sra.	*abbrev. for* **señora**
Srta.	*abbrev. for* **señorita**
suavizante *m*	hair conditioner
subterráneo(a)	underground

subtítulo *m*	subtitle
sucursal *f*	branch
suela *f*	sole
sueldo *m*	wage
suelo *m*	soil ; ground ; floor
suelto *m*	loose change *(money)*
sueño *m*	dream
suerte *f*	luck
¡buena suerte!	good luck!
sujetador *m*	bra
superficie *f*	surface ; top
superior	higher
supermercado *m*	supermarket
supositorio *m*	suppository
sur *m*	south
surf *m*	surfing
surtidor de gasolina *m*	petrol pump
tabaco *m*	tobacco
tabla *f*	board
tabla de surf	surf board
tabla de quesos	cheeseboard
tablao flamenco *m*	Flamenco show
tableta *f*	tablet ; bar *(chocolate)*
taco *m*	stuffed tortilla
tacón *m*	heel *(shoe)*
talco *m*	talc
TALGO *m*	Intercity train
talla *f*	size
tallarines *mpl*	noodles
taller *m*	workshop
talón *m*	heel *(foot)* ; counterfoil ; stub
talón bancario	cheque

también	as well ; also ; too
tampoco	neither
tampones *mpl*	tampons
tapas *fpl*	appetizers
taquilla *f*	box office ; ticket office
tarde	late
tarde *f*	evening ; afternoon
de la tarde	pm
tarifa *f*	tariff ; rate
tarjeta *f*	card
tarjeta del banco	banker's card
tarjeta de crédito	credit card
tarjeta de embarque	boarding pass
tarjeta verde	green card
tarro *m*	jar ; pot
tarta *f*	cake ; tart
tarta de almendras	almond tart
tarta helada	cake containing ice cream
tarta de nueces	walnut tart
tasca *f*	bar ; economical restaurant
taxista *m/f*	taxi driver
taza *f*	cup
té *m*	tea
teatro *m*	theatre
teleférico *m*	cablecar
telefonear	to call ; to phone
telefonista *m/f*	operator ; telephonist
teléfono *m*	phone ; telephone
telesilla *m*	ski lift ; chair lift
televisión *f*	television
Televisión Española	Spanish Television
televisor *m*	television set
temperatura *f*	temperature
temporada *f*	season
temporada alta	high season

temprano(a)	early
tener	to have
tenis *m*	tennis
tequila *f*	tequila
termómetro *m*	thermometer
ternera *f*	veal
fiambre de ternera	veal pâté
ternera al jugo	veal casserole in white wine
filete de ternera	veal steak
tiempo *m*	time ; weather
tienda *f*	store ; shop
tienda de campaña	tent
tienda de deportes	sports shop
tila *f*	lime-flower tea
timbre *m*	doorbell ; official stamp
tinto *m*	red wine
tintorería *f*	dry-cleaner's
tipo *m*	sort
tíquet *m*	ticket
tirad	pull *(on door)*
tirador *m*	handle
tirar	to throw (away) ; to pull
para tirar	disposable
tiritas *fpl*	elastoplast
toalla *f*	towel
tocar	to touch ; to play *(instrument)*
no tocar	do not touch
tocino *m*	bacon
todo(a)	all
todo	everything
todo el mundo	everyone
todo incluido	all inclusive
tomar	to take ; to have food/drink
tomate *m*	tomato
tónica *f*	tonic water

tono *m*	tone
tono de marcar	dialling tone
toquen: no toquen	please do not touch
torcedura *f*	sprain
torero *m*	bullfighter
toro *m*	bull
torre *f*	tower
torrijas *fpl*	French toast
torta *f*	cake
tortilla *f*	omelette ; thin maize pancake
tortilla española	potato and onion omelette
tortilla francesa	plain omelette
tortilla al ron	sweet rum omelette
tortilla soufflé	omelette soufflé
tos *f*	cough
tostada *f*	toast
tournedós *m*	thick slice of beef fillet
traducción *f*	translation
tráfico *m*	traffic
traje *m*	suit ; outfit
traje de etiqueta	evening dress *(man's)*
traje de noche	evening dress *(woman's)*
trampolín *m*	diving board
transbordador *m*	car ferry
transbordo *m*	transfer
en tránsito	in transit
tranvía *m*	tram ; short-distance train
tras	after ; behind
tratar con cuidado	handle with care
travesía *f*	crossing
tren *m*	train
trucha *f*	trout
trucha a la navarra	trout baked with ham
trueno *m*	thunder
trufa *f*	truffle

tumbarse	to lie down
tumbona f	deckchair
túnel m	tunnel
turista m/f	tourist
turístico(a)	tourist
turno m	turn
espere su turno	wait for your turn
turrón m	nougat
TVE	abbrev. for **Televisión Española**

Ud(s)	see usted(es)
últimamente	lately
último(a)	last
ultramarinos m	grocery shop
uña f	nail (finger, toe)
ungüento m	ointment
únicamente	only
unidad	unit
universidad f	university
unos(as)	some
urbanización f	residential development
urgencias fpl	casualty department
urgente	urgent ; express
usar	to use
uso m	use ; custom
uso externo/tópico	for external use only
usted(es)	you
útil	useful
utilizar	to use
uva f	grape
UVI	intensive care unit (hospital)

vacaciones *fpl*	holiday
vagón *m*	railway carriage
vainilla *f*	vanilla
vale *m*	token ; voucher
¡vale!	OK
válido hasta ...	valid until ...
valle *m*	valley
valor *m*	value
vapor *m*	steam
al vapor	steamed
vaqueros *mpl*	jeans
variado(a)	assorted ; mixed
varios(as)	several
vasco(a)	Basque
vaso *m*	glass
Vd(s)	*abbrev. for* usted(es)
veces *fpl*	times
vegetariano(a)	vegetarian
vehículo *m*	vehicle
vela *f*	sail ; sailing
velocidad *f*	speed
velocidad limitada	speed limit
vender	to sell
se vende	for sale
veneno *m*	poison
venir	to come
venta *f*	sale; country inn
ventana *f*	window
ventanilla *f*	window *(in car, train)*
ver	to see ; to watch
verano *m*	summer
verdad *f*	truth
¿de verdad?	really?
verdadero(a)	true ; genuine

verde	green
verduras *fpl*	vegetables
verificar	to check
versión *f*	version
versión original	original version
vespa *f*	motor scooter
vestido *m*	dress
veterinario(a) *m/f*	vet(erinary surgeon)
vez *f*	time
vía *f*	track ; rails ; platform
por vía oral/bucal	orally
viajar	to travel
viaje *m*	journey ; trip
viaje organizado	package tour
viajero *m*	traveller
vida *f*	life
vieira *f*	scallop
viejo(a)	old
viento *m*	wind
viernes *m*	Friday
viernes santo	Good Friday
vinagre *m*	vinegar
vinagreta *f*	vinaigrette *(dressing)*
vino *m*	wine
vino blanco	white wine
vino de la casa	house wine
vino dulce	sweet wine
vino de mesa	table wine
vino rosado	rosé wine
vino seco	dry wine
vino tinto	red wine
visa *f*	visa
visita *f*	visit
visitar	to visit
vista *f*	view

vitrina *f*	**shop window** (Lat. Am.)
VO (versión original)	**undubbed version** (of film)
volar	**to fly**
volumen *m*	**volume**
voltaje *m*	**voltage**
voz *f*	**voice**
vuelo *m*	**flight**
vuelta *f*	**turn ; return ; change** (money)
wáter *m*	**lavatory ; toilet**
yate *m*	**yacht**
yema *f*	**egg yolk**
yo	**I ; me**
yogur *m*	**yoghurt**
zanahoria *f*	**carrot**
zapatillas *fpl*	**slippers ; trainers**
zapato *m*	**shoe**
zarzuela *f*	**Spanish light opera**
zarzuela de mariscos	**seafood casserole**
zarzuela de pescado	**fish in a spicy sauce**
zona *f*	**zone**
zona azul	**controlled parking area**
zona restringida	**restricted area**
zumo *m*	**juice**